JOHN'S GOSPEL
&
THE RENEWAL OF THE CHURCH

D1359257

JOHN'S GOSPEL
&
THE RENEWAL OF THE CHURCH

Wes Howard-Brook

ORBIS BOOKS

Maryknoll, New York 10545

Copyright ©1997 by Wes Howard-Brook

Queries regarding rights and permissions should be addressed to: Orbis Books, P. O. Box 308, Maryknoll, New York 10545-0308.

Published by Orbis Books, Maryknoll, NY 10545-0308
Manuscript editing and typesetting by Joan Marie Laflamme

Library of Congress Cataloging-in-Publication Data

Howard-Brook, Wes.
   John's gospel & the renewal of the church   /   Wes Howard-Brook.
      p.   cm.
   ISBN 1-57075-114-5 (alk. paper)
    1. Bible.   N.T.   John—Criticism, interpretations, etc.   2. Church renewal.   I. Title.
BS2615.2.H68   1996
226.5'06—dc21   96-48412
                                      CIP

Contents

Introduction

Working the Works of the One Who Sent Jesus

As Jesus and his disciples walk through Jerusalem, they encounter an all too common sight: a blind beggar seeking alms. Somehow, they discern that the person has always been this way. They begin to wonder: whose fault is it for this one to have been born blind?

Jesus refutes the premise that underlies their inquiry. Blindness is not caused by sin. Therefore, the discipleship task is not to engage in moral argument but to be about the process of healing. He tells his confused followers, "We must work the works of the One who sent me, while it is day" (Jn 9:4).

Many in the churches of the United States find themselves in a situation similar to that of the first disciples. We look around at brokenness and suffering, violence and poverty, and inevitably fall into squabbles over who is to blame. John's gospel invites the faithful to a different course of action. It offers to teach us how to be church in a world in desperate need of healing, how to bring the Word to bear on the struggles of our time.

The synoptic gospels aim much of their discipleship energy at issues of economics. They abound with parables and dramatic scenes that challenge believers to reconsider their relationship with money and possessions. The fourth gospel, in contrast, has little to say about such topics. Instead, it offers insight into how the Christian community is to be a sign of God's love for the world (Jn 3:16, 13:34-35).

The church's memory of this Johannine function is built into the liturgical cycle throughout the seasons of Lent and Easter. Readings from John's gospel are proclaimed week after week as winter unfolds into spring, as we experience once again the victory of light over darkness (Jn 1:5). But this Easter invitation is intended to renew a process that is to be a constant element of the church's life, not simply a once-a-year occasion. The Lent and Easter readings from the fourth gospel call the church into an ongoing flow of reflection on its vocation.

The gospel itself refers to this encounter as a *crisis* (Jn 3:19, 5:22-30, etc.). It is literally a "judgment"—the meaning of the Greek word *krisis*—in which life-and-death choices must be made. Whether the church is a sign of love, which invites the world to healing and transformation, or a sign of division, which threatens to turn people away from the gospel, hangs on how we respond to this crisis daily, yearly, and over the centuries.

In our own day many internal struggles seem to paralyze the church in the moralizing mode. We haggle endlessly over the minutiae of procedure and power. Gender, ethnicity, and social status become battlegrounds on which we act out our anger and frustration. We cast blame, create enemies, and project our own fears onto the "other." We argue over whose fault it is rather than being about the business of healing.

The "good news" is that this darkness is precisely what the fourth gospel was intended to shine its light upon. Jesus, the Word of God, comes into a religious realm fighting over just these sorts of issues. Are we to rely on the teachings of those who hold offices in the religious establishment or look for wisdom in new places (Jn 3)? How can our spirituality be inclusive of a diversity of ethnic experience while remaining true to the tradition we have inherited (Jn 4)? How do "ordinary" people who have experienced the presence of the Spirit in their lives share this gift in witness before the powers (Jn 9)?

These and other questions of immediate importance to the church today echo out of the Lenten lectionary readings and into the daily life of the faith community. The passages we hear proclaimed from the fourth gospel during this season veil their wisdom in a thick mist of metaphor and irony. They offer not pithy aphorisms to be printed on prayer cards but the invitation and challenge of following the course of the fourth gospel from beginning to end. In our "sound-bite culture" this can seem like a roundabout, even frustrating process. Can't we just "cut to the chase" and skip all the narrative nuance and dramatic detail? The attempt to subvert the process of prayerful study and reflection, however, will not bear "fruit for eternal life" (Jn 4:36, cf. 15:16). It merely extends the endless battle of quotations, in which the gospel is used as a weapon to fire at those whom we perceive as the causes of "sin." The alternative process may require more initial energy but will reward us in the end with the opening of blind eyes and the emergence of life from dark tombs.

This book offers not answers but questions. It attempts to help readers concerned with the role and shape of the church in the world to penetrate the mist and to walk with the Johannine Jesus on the journey through the fourth gospel *and* through the liturgical cycle. This involves an understanding of how the fourth gospel functioned in the early church as part of the process of inviting new members into the baptismal commitment at Easter, and how that invitation called the already-baptized into reflection on their own discipleship undertaking.

The symbols of death and resurrection reach their climax on Good Friday and Easter, yet they form the foundation of the church's life throughout the year. Similarly, the Johannine lectionary stories for the Lent and Easter seasons are proclaimed at a particular time of year but provide a framework for the fullness of the church's life. Thus, we begin with consideration of the role of Lent as a call to renewal, rebirth, and recommitment to our baptismal promises.

1

Learning Again How to Read

COMING TO GRIPS WITH THE "HOW"
OF READING JOHN'S GOSPEL

One of the difficulties in attempting the plunge into the baptismal waters of John's gospel—or of any biblical text, for that matter—is the great chasm separating us from the world of Jesus and the first Christian communities. To attempt to bridge this gap, scholars over the centuries have devised many methods. In the first centuries, for example, difficult passages were often seen as allegories, wherein otherwise indecipherable symbols and situations were read as stand-ins for something more familiar from the reader's own world of experience.

Much later, with the European Enlightenment and the Age of Reason, scholars uncomfortable with "miracles" began to apply tools of the emerging scientific method to biblical texts. The task, as with much of Western scientific procedure, was to dissect the whole into numerous minuscule parts. Thus, the Jesus of Mark's gospel or of John's gospel was replaced by "the historical Jesus," an academic construction built up, like Frankenstein's beast, from patched-together parts. One consequence has been the estrangement of many believers from the Bible itself, apart from the prayerful attempt to encounter Jesus "directly" through a meditative or other spontaneous interpretation of a text. Serious Bible study is relegated, as with many other endeavors, to the realm of experts in the academic guild, whose sublime and elevated conver-

1

sations rarely come down to the thicker air of everyday church life.

Recently some academics have embarked on a quest for new reading methods. Starting with the insight that the gospels are, after all, *texts*, scholars have applied a plethora of interpretative schema derived from studies of other texts, such as the modern novel. These methods, grouped under the rubric *literary criticism*, have generated valuable insights into the meanings of the gospel narratives. However, just as with historical criticism, these reading tools easily can remain in the hands of specialists familiar with the esoterica of deconstruction, structuralism, and other intellectual nooks and crannies.

No interpreter of biblical texts can pretend to approach the task without a "method" of reading. If for no other reason than the cultural and linguistic gap between ourselves and the biblical authors and audiences, we must, at some level, come to grips with the challenge of reflecting on *how* we decide what a given text might mean. Readers interested in a more full description of my own struggle with these issues as they apply to John's gospel may find the discussion in *Becoming Children of God: John's Gospel and Radical Discipleship* (pp. 1-15) helpful. For the purpose of helping readers understand how this book comes to its conclusions, I offer the following brief summary. Readers not for the moment concerned with *how* but eager to jump to *what* may feel free to skip to the next section, where the interpretation itself begins.

THE "HOW" OF THIS BOOK'S INTERPRETATION OF JOHN'S GOSPEL

John's gospel was a text written by and for people to whom words bore sacred power. The first line of the text confronts us with this central reality: "In the beginning was the word, and the word was God." In our world of e-mail and junk mail, of thousand-page pieces of legislation and multimillion-copy novels, words can be simply a cheap resource for taking care of business. We skim more often than we actually read. We scan for the key point that we need to know, then move on to the next disposable text.

One of the first principles helpful to our encounter with John's gospel is that *every word counts*. Many passages turn on the subtle echo of a previously sounded theme. Others find their key in the presence or absence of the smallest and seemingly most insignificant words. To discover the message of John for the church today, we must discipline ourselves to become careful readers. Only by being willing to read and read again, to turn back to passages long since digested to search for previously hidden links, can we come to know the power of the narrative's sacred inscriptions.

Another element to which we must attend is the *tremendous difference in cultural understandings and practices* between first-century Palestinians and other Mediterraneans, on the one hand, and twenty-first-century North Americans, on the other. For example, our socialization leads us to revere the powerful *individual* who overcomes obstacles, resists distractions, and proceeds forward to his or her unique goal. Our spirituality is often focused on such outcomes as "personal growth," a psycho-theological translation of "success." Thus, our biblical reading tends to see opportunities to construct models of personal morality focused on aspects of "sin," which remains, apparently, the personal responsibility of each sovereign individual. During Lent, this leads us to reflect on our need for repentance over such acts as gluttony or other forms of indulgence, often expressed in sexual terms. We use the sacred season to turn *inward*, focusing on our individual struggles to overcome whatever obstacles we perceive as inhibiting our journey to our "true selves."

Tribal and village cultures, in contrast, have little conception of individual achievement. Reality is primarily *communal*. The value of each member is measured by his or her conformity to shared ideas about how to produce the common good. Growth, as an aspect of the wider notion of *change*, is an instability that can threaten to undermine the security of the community. In such a milieu individuals gain respect by maintaining expected norms. Biblical stories invite members of communities to consider how they have or have not been faithful *as a people* to the covenant. Thus, we see in the synoptic gospels that Jesus frequently directs his speech to cities (e.g., Mt 11:21-24; Lk 13:34) or refers to "the nations" as a unit (Mt 5:47; Mk 10:42). Lent, for this kind of culture, invited reflection on the community's need for repentance. It called people to turn *outward*, focusing on their common struggle to resist the ways of "the world."

A similar comparative analysis could be performed for other aspects of our cultures. Throughout this book readers will find references to these cultural differences, as they help to shed light on how these texts sounded to their first audiences.

A final principle important to this book's reading of John's gospel is *that each passage must be understood in the context of the entire text.* Accustomed as we are to a lectionary approach, which slices readings from their narrative roots, it can be a powerful experience to listen to how different a passage can sound when considered within the overall flow. While this book will not provide reflections on all of John's gospel (a task taken up in *Becoming Children of God*), the meaning of each primary passage will be constructed from an implicit understanding of the text as a whole. The exigencies of weekly worship require that we pick and choose among passages, highlighting in special seasons those of greatest power. But we risk losing that power if we fail to take a step back from time to time to see the bigger picture. A picture of George Washington or Martin Luther King, Jr., frozen in a moment of history only makes sense in the context of the larger flow of events. Similarly, the raising of Lazarus becomes most inspiring when one brings to the reading a recognition of the Judean conspiracy against Jesus looming in the background. For preachers and catechists this calls for a sensitivity to and familiarity with the broader picture than the lectionary snapshot presupposes. This book attempts to provide some of that context.

—PREACHING AND REFLECTION IDEAS—

Preaching Themes

1. Invite people to reflect not on the content of a reading but on *how* and *what* they read. Ask what they have read in the past twenty-four hours: TV listings, food packages, billboards, newspapers, road signs, telephone books, parish bulletins, and so on. Point out how many words compete for our attention

each day and the importance of setting aside time to read the stories of our ancestors in faith.

2. Share a story of one of your own reading experiences, perhaps a time when you missed the point which someone brought to your attention later or which you discovered only upon re-reading. Invite reflection on people's ways of reading and the different experiences of reading alone or in groups.

3. Consider Jesus' admonition to learn to "read the signs of the times" or Pilate's words above the cross (Jn 19:19-22). Reflect on the role of the *readings* as part of the liturgical rhythm. What readings stand out in people's minds? Do they recall a favorite homily or sermon that provided a key insight that remained with them over time?

4. Consider the role of stories in generating and animating faith among a group of people: the "big" biblical stories (Creation, the Exodus, the Passion), our Christian stories (St. Francis, the Crusades, the Reformation), our national stories (Columbus, the Founding Fathers, the Frontier), our personal stories of origin (our movement from an ancestral home to our current social location, our childhood). Reflect on how every story, including our own personal story, requires interpretation and reshaping to fit later situations.

Small Group Activities

1. Distribute a copy of the day's newspaper among the group. Have each person pick a story that says something to him or her and ask each person to report on the story in one minute or less. After each person has retold a story, take some quiet time to consider how his or her report *interpreted* the newspaper story according to certain assumptions, for example, the accuracy of the information, the degree of objectivity of the author, the understanding of cultural metaphors or euphemisms contained in the story that might sound odd to cultural outsiders, the degree of sympathy of the reader with the situation or point of view reflected in the story. Allow time for brief sharing of what each person discovered about his or her read-

ing assumptions. If time permits, repeat the exercise with a *brief* biblical passage.

2. Pick a reading from the Bible that is unlikely to be familiar to most members of the group, for example; a piece of legislation from Leviticus or Deuteronomy or a story of a less well-known monarch from the books of Kings. Read it slowly aloud as a group. After each verse make a list (on a whiteboard, flip chart, overhead—something all can see) of whatever questions come to mind about the reading: the location of obscure geographic settings, the cultural practices involved, the place of the reading in the larger book in which it is contained, the reasons for a character's words or action, and so on.

   When the list is complete, consider what implicit reading method underlies each question. For example, asking about when a king lived or if an event "really happened" might suggest a *historical* method; asking about why a character says or does something or why the author included or excluded something might suggest a *literary* method. Invite the participants to consider why they asked the questions they did and what this might suggest about their presuppositions about the Bible as "history," "literature," "God's word," or some other preconceived category.

3. Pick a reading from the Bible that is likely to be familiar to all participants, for example, a Lenten scrutiny reading from John's gospel. Have each person consider what preexisting interpretations of the reading he or she holds before the story is read. Allow a brief period to share some of these interpretations (without commenting on the sharings or engaging in argument about the "right" interpretation). Then follow the procedure in Activity 2 above. Ask each person to consider how the gathering of questions has shed new light on his or her preexisting interpretation. Allow time to share these new insights.

Reflection Questions

1. *Personal:* What assumptions do I make about the Bible before I start to read a particular passage—that it is God's word?

that it is historically accurate? that it contains collections of stories that reflect particular cultural situations? others?

2. *Social and cultural:* What assumptions are prevalent about the Bible in this country? in this region of the country? in this city or locality? in this neighborhood? in this household? If I don't know what assumptions are common in a given sector of society, how might I find out? How do my assumptions fit or diverge from the dominant cultural assumptions?

3. *Ecclesial:* What teachings does my church provide about how to read the Bible? How might these teachings be different from other churches' teachings about the Bible? How are such teachings reinforced in practice? What happens when or if there is conflict between a given church teaching and a person's or group's interpretation, for example, about women's role in church/society, gay/lesbian acceptance, the role of the Bible in the realm of public discourse?

2

Preparing for the Journey

John 1:1-18

The "road map" for any travel with the Johannine Jesus is found in the first poetic passage, commonly known as the Prologue. There are many different ways to envision the structure of the poem. The division set out below shows the text organized as a "*chiasm*" (see *Becoming Children of God* for chiastic outlines of the entire gospel of John). Although foreign at first to our way of reading, chiasm was a common way of organizing texts in the ancient world, including the Bible. The Prologue chiasm functions by drawing our attention to the center of the passage, giving us a clue with which to interpret the entire passage.

Chiasm: John 1:1-18

A: 1-5: relationship of Logos to God, creation, humanity
   B: 6-8: witness of John the Baptist (negative)
      C: 9-11: journey of light/Logos (negative)
         D: 12-13: gift of authority to become children of God
      C¹: 14: journey of Logos (positive)
   B¹: 15: witness of John the Baptist (positive)
A¹: 16-8: relationship of Logos to humanity, re-creation (Law), God

In the chiasm shaping the Prologue, we are called to focus on the issue of *birth*. Considered in linear fashion, John's Prologue has traditionally been read as celebrating the "high Christology" of the gospel. That is, the introductory proclamation that "the Word was with God, and the Word was God," has been taken to announce that Jesus-the-Word is and has always been divine. While there is no doubt that the Prologue has much to say about the Word—*logos* in Greek—a chiastic reading draws our attention away from Jesus and to the question of *discipleship.*

The first discipleship theme presented is that of *receiving* the incarnate Word, whose fleshly presence is proclaimed in 1:14. Immediately, the mythical and historical aspects of the text are intertwined. From the cosmic introductory verses linking the Word with God's creative action in Genesis 1, the text's focus narrows down to the particular moment of the earthly life of the Word. The Word "came into his own, and his own did not receive him." The primal sin among believers from the Johannine perspective is refusal of hospitality.

We should not be too quick to fill in the poetic blank left by the nonspecific reference to "his own." Of course, the obvious answer is the Jews, the religious/ethnic origin group of Jesus of Nazareth. But as we shall see, the gospel will not hesitate in its own time to name Jesus' opponents. And we may be surprised to find that the modern term *Jews* does not accurately describe the nature of those who are deemed guilty of this failure of hospitality.

For now, the Prologue switches away from the opponents to those favored by the narrative, those who *did* receive the Word. Because of this reception, the favored ones are given an unfathomable gift: "authority to become children of God." To the extent that John's gospel presents a positive description of Jesus as "son of God," we must recognize that it offers to would-be disciples a parallel relationship with the One it calls Father (see also, 15:9, 20:21).

The gift is conditional on two more factors in addition to the provision of hospitality to the Word. Verse 12 states that the gifted were "the ones believing/trusting in his name." This condition will be echoed near the end of the gospel, when the narrator names the reason the gospel was written: "so that you may believe that Jesus is the Messiah, the son of God, and so that believing/trusting, you may be having life in his name" (20:31). Together, we find the Prologue and the near conclusion inviting readers ("you") into the same relationship that the first disciples had with Jesus. The invitation to and support of this relationship is the key to the role John's gospel seeks to play in the life of the church.

The Greek verb *pisteuo*, which is usually translated "to believe," can also mean "to trust." The sought-for relationship is not a matter of intellectual assent or of calling upon Jesus' name as a magic talisman. Instead, the gospel introduces here another of its central themes: inviting people into a *communion of trust.* To be among those "believing/trusting in his name" is to put one's life in the hands of the community that proclaims and lives the Word. As Jesus was betrayed by one of his own (13:21), so too the members of the Johannine community experienced the wrenching horror of the breach of trust among friends (1 Jn 2:19). All those who dare to join hearts in a way of life rejected and ridiculed by the world face this risk yet are ever needful of the support that can be found only within a community sharing a common faith.

The final factor involved in distinguishing those who are authorized to become children of God is found in 1:13: they are "born from God." What this might mean is stated negatively by comparing it to three rejected birth alternatives: "from blood," "from the will of flesh," and "from the will of a man." These three form the thematic core of the scrutinies, the process of reflection, purification, and exorcism to which catechumens—and the whole church—are invited during the third, fourth, and fifth weeks of Lent. The lesson of "will of a man" will be learned in the first scrutiny's reading, the story of the Samaritan woman (Jn 4). The second scrutiny reading—John 9, the person healed of blind birth—will engage the issue of birth from "will of flesh," picking up themes introduced in Jesus' dialogue with Nicodemus in John 3. Finally, blood-birth will be considered in the third scrutiny, the various reactions recorded to the death of Lazarus in John 11.

With this understanding of the place of discipleship at the center of the Prologue—and therefore, at the center of the gospel—we can return to the beginning of the text to note a few more themes that are introduced at the start of the narrative.

John's gospel most likely was written for a community of believers near the end of the first century, at least two generations after Jesus' ministry. Reactions to the expanding Christian claims for Jesus' authority began to harden among the discipleship community's opponents. We see the parallel movement of Jesus' followers under persecution and of their persecutors acted out in the drama of John 9. What at first must have seemed to be a traditional argument among discipleship groups over whose teacher was holier eventually degenerated into outright hatred and violence. In being pushed to the theological wall by their questioners, Jesus' followers moved from proclaiming their leader "teacher" and "prophet" to more exalted—and politically charged—titles such as "messiah." While the synoptics and Paul record the affirmation of Jesus as "messiah" (Christ), only John's gospel takes this progression the next and final step. Jesus, more than Moses or John the Baptist or any of the ancient prophets, embodies God in human form. This awesome proclamation is sounded from the first verses, framing the Prologue with its grandeur and audacity. It is an "in your face" claim, which would put off many readers and hearers before a single story was told. From the gospel's perspective, such a confrontational style is a necessary aspect of shocking people into *krisis*, the moment in which judgment takes place. The presence of the Word in the world takes people by surprise, upsetting their complacency and self-created (false) sense of security. By poetically, if boldly, laying out its cards from the start, the gospel attempts to wake us from our somnolence and to allow ourselves to be broken open by God's creative *and* judgmental Word.

In choosing the metaphors and images it does, the gospel consciously puts itself into conversation with the Hebrew scriptures, the texts which would be known to the Jewish audience as the "word of God." As 1:1 echoes Genesis with its announcement of God's creative power exercised through speech, so the end of the Prologue takes up the issue of Moses, the traditional bearer, if not author, of the first books of the Bible.

The first scriptural metaphor, "word of God," became a richly complex symbol when translated into the Greek of the first century as *logos*. The term had many nuances in secular and philosophical Greek, some of which were adapted by Jewish-Hellenistic writers to explain their tradition to gentile intellectuals. Thus, Philo of Alexandria, a near contemporary of the gospel writer(s), used *logos* to refer both to God's word and to the more philosophical principles of reason, rationality, and order so treasured by the Greek thinkers. The work of Philo and others took creative advantage of the linguistic commonality between a central Hebrew and Greek concept. John's gospel used it to present the Incarnate One as embodying the highest notions of which its audience, whether Jew or gentile, could conceive.

The second scriptural metaphor comes from the Moses tradition: *torah*, translated into Greek as *nomos*, and into English as *law*. It is all too easy for latter-day Christians unfamiliar with the Hebrew scriptures and with Jewish practice—both ancient and modern—to caricature Torah and its practitioners as sterile and ossified rules and rule-keepers, suitable for entombment. Some of this comes from difficulty of translation and some from ease of implicit anti-Judaism. Neither is satisfactory as a reaction to the gospel's challenge to its original opponents or to its more recent ones. *Torah*, better translated as "instruction," was and remains a living reality for Jews. One of the primary narrative opponent-groups of Jesus in the gospels is the Pharisees, who were renounced by their more conservative (and socially elite) Jewish brethren for their promotion of "oral Torah" as a supplement to the books of the Pentateuch. It was precisely the Pharisees' claims that Torah—God's instruction to humanity—could not be bound in a book that led them to be seen as formidable opponents by the early Christians.

The problem the gospel addresses, then, is not the bankruptcy of Torah, and certainly not the supposed legalism of "Judaism." Rather, *the problem is a hierarchical religious institution's attempt to control interpretation of the sacred texts through its enforcement of a violent and oppressive cultic system*, at the price of leaving the world in "darkness." This theme will return throughout the Lenten readings, as Jesus confronts the hypocrisy, fear, blindness, and self-glorification of those in official authority. Thus, the Prologue ends in 1:18 with its claim that God is *only* "explained" by the One who is in an intimate relationship with God. It is the failure of the Judean religious establishment and its supporters to allow the tradition to speak to the concrete needs of ordinary people that is pilloried by the gospel.

The consequence of this sin is that the world remains in darkness. The mission of the Word, both in the incarnate Jesus and in the life of the church throughout history, is to "shine in the darkness" but not to allow itself to be "overpowered" by that darkness (1:5; 17:14-15). The Prologue thus introduces the gospel's challenge to the church not to seek safety by withdrawal from the dark world but to trust in the light, which cannot be extinguished by the worst that evil has to offer.

The attempt to seek refuge in a holy community apart from the "taint" of the world was and remains an illusion. The Qumran community, famous for its production and protection of the texts known as the Dead Sea Scrolls, attempted this approach during a span of some two hundred years preceding and following Jesus. Its own documents were filled with apocalyptic anger and expectation for God's powerful destruction of the corrupt elements that had taken control of Jerusalem, a jihad long predating Islamic notions of holy war. At the same time, it is clear that the Qumranians came to recognize that sin could not be barred at the door: it resided in each human heart, whether living in the holy city or in the desert. In our day we find survivalists, militias, and other groups on the militarist side of the ledger, and communal farms and wilderness communities on the nonviolent wing. Both, to the extent that they have given up on the possibility of the world's conversion, manifest their own lack of faith in the God who sent Jonah to Nineveh preaching repentance. For Christians attempting to put the gospel into practice, withdrawal for a time may provide an opportunity for prayer and healing, but it cannot be where life is lived. The church's journey may lead into the desert, but it then calls the community of faith back to witness to God's promise of love among the brokenhearted and their oppressors.

—PREACHING AND REFLECTION IDEAS—

Preaching Themes

1. Reflect on the notion of *birth*. What does it mean to come into being as a new creation? Contrast the lack of choice in our natural birth with the volitional aspects of our spiritual birth. What barriers/gates prevent or invite us to enter into a reality different from that of our natural birthplace?

2. Imagine calling ourselves "children of God." Is such a title earned or given as a gift? If Jesus is the son of God, what might it mean to call ourselves sons and daughters of God? Reflect on the fine lines between self-confidence and messiah-complexed, low self-esteem and modesty. Dare we accept the invitation to develop a relationship with God of equal magnitude and dignity to Jesus' own relationship with the One he called Father?

3. Consider the idea that God acts through speech. By the power of word(s), the United States came into being. We name our children and give them a unique identity. We give ourselves labels (Catholic/Protestant, African-American, Baby Boomers, wife/husband) that create a reality about ourselves. Similarly, God is re-membered (that is, both *recalled* and *put back together*) in the church through words.

4. Consider what "word of God" we are: as individuals, as a faith community, as a broader cultural or religious unit. Do we think of ourselves as enfleshing God's word in our own unique call to live life in the world?

Small Group Activities

1. Take some quiet time for each person to recall when he or she first felt called to make a commitment to the Christian journey, either through baptism, confirmation, or other sense of decision. Invite people to share their feelings, thoughts, and stories about that moment and what led up to that moment in their lives.

2. Brainstorm possible meanings of the negative births listed in John 1:13 and list them so all can see. If part of an ongoing group, keep the list to compare it with thoughts developed during subsequent reflection on the scrutiny readings. Discuss which of those meanings would have made sense during the time in which the gospel was first proclaimed and which make sense in our own time.

3. Consider our attitudes toward "the world." Do we conceive of it as basically positive, basically negative, or a mixture of both? Discuss what it might mean to "witness to the light" as

John the Baptist did. Invite individual sharing about a time when each person felt called to witness to his or her faith in a place of darkness, that is, where that witness was not received with open arms. How did it feel? What responses were there? What happened to the relationship between witnesser and witnessee after that experience?

Reflection Questions

1. *Personal:* Do I experience myself as a son or daughter of God? If so, is it a matter of simply being human or of trying to live life in a particular way? If not, what stands in the way of my claiming such a role or title for myself?

2. *Social and cultural:* What birth images does our society generate and seek our commitment to? Examples: become a "new man" or "new woman" by driving a particular car; "start over again" with a new career.

3. *Ecclesial:* How does the church—locally, nationally, and universally—carry out the role of shining light in the darkness?

3

To Be Born from God

John 2:23–3:21, 7:45-52

The first scrutiny reading comes with the third Sunday of Lent, the story of Jesus' encounter with the Samaritan woman at the well. Before the gospel narrative relates this scene in John 4, it prepares us for it with a contrasting encounter between Jesus and Nicodemus in John 3. To appreciate the power of the watery witness in Samaria, we must first consider a darker exchange in Jerusalem.

THE MESSIAH COMES INTO THE WORLD

Between the Prologue and John 3, the gospel has charged forward into its account of Jesus' messianic ministry. It began with the official interrogation of John the Baptist across the Jordan, a site legally outside Judea's jurisdiction. The inquisitional party is made up of Temple authorities (priests and Levites), who are sent forth by the "Judeans . . . from Jerusalem."

Who are these Judeans who are established from the outset as the hostile questioners? The Greek word *Ioudaioi*, usually translated "Jews," basically refers to people of Judea, the southern province of Palestine in which Jerusalem is found. But it is not Jews who are the opponents of Jesus, for Jesus and his first disciples are quite clearly Jewish themselves. In an attempt to avoid the seemingly powerful and embarrassing anti-Jewish tone of the gospel, some scholars suggest an interpretation limited to "Jewish authorities." This ruse solves the ecumenically minded scholarly concern by limiting the gospel's anti-Jewishness to some Jews from a distant past, rather than the traditional Christian interpretation that read the gospel as an excuse for ongoing ethnic and religious prejudice bordering on the genocidal.

However, when we read the text as a whole, we find another, and more compelling option. John the Baptist's opponents from Jerusalem are all persons identified with and defensive of the status quo in Judea. Sometimes in the gospel, as here, this likely refers to the Sanhedrin and its socially elite supporters in Jerusalem and environs. Other times, it means "ordinary" people whose "birth" is from the dominant culture ("born of the will of the flesh," see chapter 5, below), the one in which the Jerusalem Temple and its ideology are deemed holy. This would include merchants and even Judean peasants whose livelihood is dependent on the maintenance of Judea (Jerusalem) as the center of Jewish religiosity and its concomitant economic power. Thus, it is both *a geographic term*, specific to the politics and economics of first-century Palestine, and a *symbolic term*, with classic significance. Therefore, near the end of the gospel, when Pilate asks Jesus—sarcastically, from Pilate's perspective—whether he (Pilate) is a Judean, the gospel's answer may well be "yes!"

As a symbol available across time and culture, "Judeans" continues to bear power. In Washington, D.C., for example, whether or not one works for the government or even cares a whit about politics, one almost certainly wants more federal power and spending if one is trying to feed a family or achieve "success" in the world's terms. Many regions in North America have similar relationships with socioeconomic powers: Detroit with the auto industry, Seattle with Boeing, southern Louisiana with petrochemicals, and so forth. Anyone who publicly opposes the will of a dominant local power will be seen as deviant and will be demonized. For Jesus to come to Jerusalem and attack the system of Temple economics is to put himself immediately in this category.

But this is to jump start the story a bit. John the Baptist is not described as himself going to Jerusalem, but he is willing to give truthful testimony when the representatives of the dominant culture come to him to challenge his "unofficial" ministry. He thus models discipleship in anticipation of the story of the person born blind, the second scrutiny reading. Rather than playing the messianic forerunner, Elijah, as he is cast in the synoptic gospels (e.g., Mk 1:6-8, 9:11-13), John is the Isaian "voice in the wilderness" (Is 40:3; Jn 1:23) who witnesses to the coming of the apocalyptic "Lamb of God."

John's insistent testimony is that he is not himself the messiah, that he serves only to witness to his presence in the world. The gospel portrays John the Baptist as dutifully subservient to the Lamb, in order to undermine the ongoing allegiance of many to the Baptizer even after Jesus has come on the scene (3:23, 4:1). Historically it seems likely that both John and Jesus continued to gather and teach disciples simultaneously. The gospel makes clear that even John understood his role as penultimate in the presence of the Lamb.

"Lamb of God" as a choice of symbols identifies the One who is to come as both a sacrificial presence (Lv 16) and as God's avenging agent (e.g., Rv 17:14). While the synoptics reserve their association of Jesus with the Passover lamb until Holy Thursday and Good Friday, John's gospel presents Jesus this way before he has even entered the story.

A symbolic week follows (1:29, 35, 43; 2:1) in which the transition from John to Jesus, from the witness to the Word, is completed. It is the week of new creation, the gospel's reconstruction of the opening chapter of Genesis. It is a new time, a new scripture, that beckons. God's Word is once again active in history!

Before Jesus comes to Jerusalem, he gathers his first disciples together. Significantly, Jesus names Simon "Peter" immediately (1:42) but does not actually call Simon to "follow" until Peter has come to know something about his own darkness (21:19). After that, Jesus provides the first clue to the new insiders that his mission in the world is supported by cosmic powers (1:51).

Unlike the synoptic gospels, which narrate a single trip to Jerusalem at the end of Jesus' life, John's gospel tells of four sojourns to the symbolic center of Israel. Unafraid of official wrath and in control of his destiny at all times, the Johannine Jesus freely travels back and forth as the Spirit moves him. His ministry oscillates between the call to gather community and heal persons, usually outside Judea (constructive), and the call to speak and perform prophetic deeds of truth-telling against the "world," headquartered in Jerusalem (disruptive).

Jesus' first journey to the Judean capital is prepared by his performance of a powerful messianic act, one perceived not by the elite but by the servants (2:9).The story of the wedding wine at Cana in Galilee announces Jesus' messianic ministry in terms comprehensible to both Jew and gentile. For Galilean Jews, prophetic promises are fulfilled (Is 62:4-5; Am 9:13-14).

For Hellenistic gentiles, a different idyllic image is invoked: that of Dionysian joy being celebrated with huge outpourings of wine. Cana was well known for its location near the legendary birthplace of Dionysus, and the region housed numerous Dionysian temples and shrines. Thus, the initial sign that Jesus performs speaks to those with eyes to see, whether Jew or Greek: the One from Nazareth is indeed a messenger from Above.

The Cana story provides an image of what earthly life in the messianic age could be: a joyous celebration overflowing with the bounty of the earth shaped by the work of human hands. But implicit in the narrative of celebration is a harsh social criticism. The water-made-wine was first contained in jars intended to be used in fulfillment of Judean purification requirements (2:6). The messianic age, just as the Prologue suggests, transcends the Judean legal rituals that had become a weak substitute for covenant life. No longer able to provide sustenance for celebration, the water jars are converted by Jesus into wine bottles. The feastmaster's comments to the bridegroom underscore this theme: "You have reserved the fine wine until this moment" (2:10). God's greatest gift to humanity has come to be, not in Jerusalem where the prophets predicted, but in Cana of Galilee.

The hint of criticism in the Cana story is brought to center stage in the second half of the diptych formed by the combined Cana and Temple exorcism narratives in John 2. Before messianic joy can truly be released into the world, Jesus must act *radically*; that is, he must get to the root of the problem (Latin *radix*, "root"). In strong contrast to the synoptics, who present Jesus' angry entry into the Temple as a proximate cause of his death sentence (e.g., Mk 11:15-18), John's gospel shifts the story to the beginning. The twofold mission of Jesus—and of his followers, then and now—is presented as a tightly woven whole. One half was revealed at Cana: the possibility of life in true harmony among humans and the earth. The second half comes in Jerusalem: the public dismantling of systems of power that have subverted God's intention for creation.

Jesus' dramatic act of civil disobedience on Passover understandably provokes the wrath of the Judeans, who challenge Jesus' authority (2:18). His response and the narrator's comments are the first indication that the Word is only understood after the experience of death and resurrection. To Judeans, *temple* means a building constructed over a lifetime by human labor. To Jesus and the post-Easter community of disciples, *temple* is the holy chamber of a fleshly body in which God can be found (2:18-22).

Only John's gospel includes among those "exorcised" from the Temple the cattle and sheep, the intended victims of the sacrificial cult in Jerusalem with which the Judean elite mystify their claim to divine authorization. Jesus' action saves the animals from their fate as fodder for the priestly power game. No longer will God's people need to rely on such acts of sacred violence to remain bonded together. It is the first intimation in the story that the community will be united through loving self-sacrifice rather than scapegoating violence (e.g., 13:14-15, 15:12-14; cf. 21:15-19).

We discover in this scene that the Word is a presence that brings people together and divides them from one another at the same time. Those who seek to walk in the light must learn, as the disciples slowly did, to read the text of life more deeply than official interpretations allow. Jesus' symbolic shutdown of Temple commerce tore down the divine canopy with which the Judeans had shrouded the gilded building. Similarly, the lesson learned by the disciples who witnessed Jesus' act should lead us to respond boldly to the false cover stories protecting our own would-be holy ground. A cursory glance at the daily newspaper or the nightly TV provides numerous opportunities for penetration of the sacred shield with which our political, corporate, and religious institutions are secured.

NICODEMUS:
TO BE BORN "NOT OF THE WILL OF FLESH"*

Following the diptych linking the Cana and Temple stories is another pair of scenes that takes us into the heart of the gospel's

---

*This is part 1 of a theme that will be continued in John 9 (see chapter 5).

challenge to the status quo. The characters Nicodemus and the Samaritan woman could hardly be more polar opposites:

	Nicodemus	Samaritan Woman
gender	male	female
homeland	Jerusalem (honored)	Sychar (dishonored)
name	provided three times	not provided
role	ruler, teacher	water carrier, "woman"
time of encounter	night	midday
primary response	"how is this possible?"	"could this be the messiah?"

In these paired stories the gospel opens up our hearts and minds to two of the "nots" of the Prologue's core. With Nicodemus comes the challenge to be born "not of the will of the flesh." With the Samaritan woman, we will be invited to be born "not of the will of a man."

The fleshly nature of Nicodemus's spirit is suggested before he even comes onto the Johannine stage. After the response to the Temple exorcism at the end of John 2 is the narrator's summary of Jesus' attitude toward those present in Jerusalem for the Passover feast. The following translation attempts to recover the original sense of the transition:

> But when he was in Jerusalem for the Passover feast, many trusted in his name, having seen the signs that he was doing. But Jesus was not entrusting himself to them, because he knew them all, and because he had no need for anyone to bear witness about a person, for he knew what was in a *person.*
>
> Now there was a *person* out of the Pharisees, Nicodemus by name, a ruler of the Judeans . . . (Jn 2:23-3:1).

Sign-faith is not trusted by Jesus (cf. 4:48). He knows that people are easily influenced by flash and power, a lesson well understood by the manipulators of political and military image-events in our own day. The pull exerted by such pyrotechnics can weaken as quickly as the fading flash itself. Jesus' mistrust expresses an initial understanding of the difference between religious thrill seekers and true pilgrims who are willing to abandon all to follow. It is just this challenge that confronts the Judean ruler as he approaches the teacher from Galilee. And, the narrator suggests, Nicodemus is precisely one of those people impressed by Jesus' powerful acts, as he himself states in 3:2.

To understand the challenge with which Jesus confronts Nicodemus and many would-be disciples, we must look very carefully at how the gospel shapes the story. To start, we should note the multifaceted introduction of this character. In addition to being a person at the Passover feast curious about Jesus' sign-making authority, we are informed of three other aspects of his social location. First, Nicodemus is a *Pharisee.* He is a member of the same group that sent inquisitors to John the Baptist on "the other side." The gospel of John relentlessly characterizes the Pharisees as ruthless opponents of Jesus and his disciples, grounding their opposition in their perception that he is a law-breaker and a blasphemer. However, underlying this public rationale, the gospel identifies the true reason for their opposition as the defense of their own worldly power (11:48). When we reach the second part of the gospel's challenge to be born "not of the will of flesh" in John 9, their collective personality will be characterized as blind to the ways of God in the world.

This harsh gospel portrait is one developed from painful experience. Before the destruction of the Jerusalem Temple by the Romans in 70 C.E. as the final crushing blow to the Judean dream of liberation, the Pharisees had been simply one group among many vying for power and influence among the intelligentsia of Palestine. Although the gospel data alone might suggest that the Pharisees were legalistic conservatives, it is important to understand that in reality they were just the opposite.

The Jewish historian Josephus describes the Pharisees more as what we might call liberals. For example, in contrast with the reactionary Sadducees, who were zealous defenders of the social status quo and the religious canopy that legitimated it, the Pharisees advocated radical changes in the site and practice of Jewish piety. Whereas the Sadducees emphasized the exclusive authority of the written Torah as interpreted by the priestly elite, the Pharisees claimed the divine authority of oral Torah, interpretable by their own rabbis. Further, whereas the Sadducees located religious practice in Temple and synagogue, the Pharisees brought religion into the daily life of home and field. One implication was that the Pharisees' system opened up the pursuit of Jewish piety to women, whose social site was the home. Finally, whereas the Sadducees emphasized the finality of earthly reality—which legitimated their own social elite status grounded in wealth and land ownership—the Pharisees accepted the relatively recent doctrine of resurrection from the dead, which opened up the possibility of post-death reversal of judgment. Thus, if one were to correlate the Pharisees' political and social stance with categories familiar to modern U.S. citizens, one might name them the liberal Democrats of their day. They advocated change on behalf of the poor, but *always from within the established religious system*, perceived as divinely authorized.

The caricature of the Pharisees in the gospels, and in John's gospel in particular, is one that evolves from the post-70 C.E. situation. After the destruction of the Temple, the priestly elite and their collaborators were rendered immediately irrelevant. Unlike the aftermath of the first Temple destruction six centuries earlier, in which the priestly establishment found itself in power in place of the delegitimated monarchy, Judea's priesthood, perhaps ironically, was never to rise from the dead. Instead, the Pharisees became the central bearers of the tradition precisely because of their location of God in text rather than Temple. The oral Torah quickly became written in the form known as the Talmud, with the Pharisees and their rabbinical successors as interpreters.

It was in this situation that the gospel felt the need to portray the Pharisees as rigid, legalistic, and blind. The Pharisees' system was the primary theological alternative to the emerging Christian churches for many of the Jewish poor in Palestine and beyond. The encounter between Nicodemus and Jesus presents the gospel's satirical version of the nature of the difference between the two approaches to holiness.

Another characteristic of Nicodemus is his portrayal as a "ruler of the Judeans." This designation can only mean that he was a member of the Jerusalem Sanhedrin, the ruling council allowed a measure of autonomy by Rome to order internal Jewish life. Of course, to protect its limited power the Sanhedrin would never be able openly to advocate resistance to Rome. This put the Sanhedrin at odds with the vast majority of Jewish Palestinians, who faced crushing Roman taxation that, in addition to the tithing tax required by Torah and its elite interpreters, annually threatened to confront the peasants with loss of land and ultimately with starvation. Thus, for that segment of the gospel's audience—at least those old enough to remember the pre-70 C.E. situation—

this aspect of Nicodemus's social location would be negatively received.

Finally, Nicodemus comes to Jesus "at night." For a gospel presenting Jesus as the light which shines in the darkness, Nicodemus's choice to approach Jesus under cover ironically reveals his at best ambiguous interest in Jesus. Near the end of John 3 the gospel emphasizes this ambiguity:

> This is the basis for the judgment: that the Light has come into the world and people loved the darkness rather than the light, for their works were evil. Everyone practicing vile deeds hates the light and does not come to the light, so that that one's works will not be reproved. But the one doing the truth does come to the light so that it may be revealed that that one's works have been done in God (Jn 3:19-21).

Nicodemus has indeed "come to the light." But whether his deeds match his curiosity is left wide open.

The Pharisee's initial address to Jesus suggests that he considers the Galilean to be one of his own, a rather shocking beginning given Jesus' disruptive attitude toward the status quo. He offers Jesus the honorable title of rabbi, which otherwise would have been a hard-earned sign of respect from one trained and approved by his predecessors in Torah interpretation and practice. Further, Nicodemus speaks in the first person plural, suggesting that he comes as a representative of other Judean Pharisees. His initial statement continues to offer Jesus unexpected praise, claiming to "know" that Jesus has "come from God as teacher" and that "God is with him."

What was Nicodemus expecting with this conversation starter? Contrary to the negative markers provided by the narrator, Nicodemus's own words seem to establish his inquiry as sincere, even startlingly open to the possibility of Jesus' prophetic, if not messianic, nature. Yet he neither asks a question nor proposes a Torah conundrum, as would be an expected way to engage a rabbi in discussion.

Custom would suggest that Jesus respond in kind, with honorable affirmation of Nicodemus's own authority and status. However, rather than engage in the culturally expected exchange, Jesus puts a solemn challenge directly to the Judean ruler: "Unless one is born *anōthen*, one cannot see the reign of God." The use of the Greek *anōthen* creates an exquisite double entendre, unpreservable in English translation. The word means both "again" and "from above." The word play sets up a characteristic Johannine opportunity for misunderstanding by Jesus' conversation partner, a situation repeated in the encounter at the well in Samaria in John 4.

Whatever Jesus meant by the figure of speech, Nicodemus can hear only its absurdly literal meaning. His double question in response ironically reveals the nature of his problem. His social status and Pharisaic training have not prepared him for the possibility of God acting in a new way, one with dire implications for all that Nicodemus holds precious.

Jesus' second statement ignores Nicodemus's confused questions and comes at the issue with another figure of speech: birth through water and spirit. From the earliest post-biblical days Jesus' image has been associated with baptism into the Christian community. It is here we find John's gospel operating out of its bifurcated sense of time. For Nicodemus, an inquirer early in Jesus' ministry, the image cannot possibly be understood in this way, although it *would* be possible for him to understand it in relation to John's baptism (1:26). For the gospel's late-first-century audience, though, the invitation/challenge would be crystal clear. The equation new birth=Christian baptism would suggest to listeners the scope of what is demanded by the presence of the Word in the world.

We should also note that Jesus' two statements also change the terms of relationship with the reign of God. The first invites "seeing," while the second invites "entering." The implication is that without the transformation of heart and social situation required by new birth, even perceiving the existence of God's reign is impossible. The second figure of speech indicates the way in which the new birth takes place: through preparation for and commitment to the community of Jesus' followers.

Jesus continues his speech to Nicodemus with still another metaphor, drawing out the meaning of birth in "spirit." The ways of the world are characterized as "flesh," something transitory, subject to decay, and limited in movement. In contrast, the Christian community is characterized as born from spirit, something elusive, limitless, and eternal. One should be careful not to read Jesus' admonition as counseling against created bodiliness. The gospel affirms the divine source of creation to such an extent that the Word becomes flesh (1:14). It is not criticism of creation that is at issue, but condemnation of thinking and being "from below," that is, according to human-made order. Unlike the Pharisees' religious system, the Christian source is "from above" and cannot be contained within a person or a text.

The implications of Jesus' image remain powerful today. For those practicing Christianity within the institutional structure of a church, the image reminds us that God's spirit cannot be bounded by *any* religious system. When the Spirit blows onto a person or faith community, people may not understand how or why that person or community was chosen, just as the prophets of old, including Moses, disclaimed the desire or worthiness of bearing God's word (e.g., Ex 3:10-12; Jer 4:1-10). But the Spirit does blow nonetheless, with no respect for human social distinctions, offices, or resumés.

Thus, Jesus confronts Nicodemus with a two-part challenge. First, to see or enter God's reign, one must be willing to be baptized into the community of Jesus' followers. This step is equivalent to being born again/from above: it requires starting life over, leaving behind one's previous commitments and worldly honor, and making a commitment to the new community. Second, it requires acceptance of God's freedom, which can bring about newness in unexpected ways.

Sadly, all the Judean ruler can do in response to this invitation is express his dumbfounded wonder at the possibility (3:9). Jesus' word has taken him by surprise and created a crisis, a moment in which Nicodemus is put to the test. To accept Jesus' challenge would be to give up all that he has worked hard to become, all that previously seemed blessed by God.

And yet, Jesus does expect Nicodemus to be able to respond positively to the challenge. He brings the conversation full circle, with a twist. Where Nicodemus addresses Jesus as a "teacher sent from God," Jesus addressed him as "teacher of Israel," that is, one holding the office of teacher in the religious institution. In effect, Jesus tells him, "there is enough in the tradition we share that speaks to the truth of what I have said. You *should* know this without my telling you so!"

But Nicodemus has no more to say during this scene. Instead, Jesus begins to speak in the plural, on behalf of the community gathered around this Word. He speaks to their experience, late in the first century, of attempting to enlighten their Jewish brothers and sisters about the truth of their tradition, which had become encrusted over time with "religion." But by that time misunderstandings about Jesus had hardened into personal hostility and prejudice against Jesus-followers. Just to mention the name Jesus was to invoke strong feelings, often incapable of penetration by prayerful discussion. The witness offered in love was rejected, along with the bearers of that witness. Nicodemus's silence speaks loudly to the failure of those sympathetic to Jesus to speak up against the injustice and violence done in the name of God to those claiming the name of Jesus.

Nicodemus's silence results, however, not from concern over the controversy of using Jesus' name (which is rarely used by the opponents in the gospel: 6:42; 18:5, 7; 19:19), but from an emerging recognition of the cost of discipleship. In a U.S. culture where human-generated honor and standards of "success" rule the day, it is very easy for many to identify with Nicodemus's dilemma. When a group with whom I spent two years studying John's gospel on a weekly basis decided to celebrate our conclusion with a "John's gospel costume party" at which people were invited to come as their favorite gospel character, nearly half came as Nicodemus! As people on the top of the world's pyramid of privilege, we recognized the challenge of letting go of all that the world deems worthy of seeking and celebrating. It is not until John 9 that we discover the only incentive that can support us in taking such a risky step. But first, we must follow Nicodemus, who is given two more chances in the gospel to take the step for himself.

NICODEMUS'S CHALLENGE TO BE BORN *ANŌTHEN*

Much later in the gospel, after the Judeans have begun to seek Jesus' death, Nicodemus comes upon the stage once more. In 7:32, after the Pharisees and chief priests overhear the Jerusalem crowd speculating about the possibility of Jesus' messiahship, they send out the police to bring Jesus in. But when the police return empty handed in 7:45, their dispatchers turn on them: "You have not been misled too, have you? No one from the rulers or the Pharisees have believed in him, have they?" Their sarcastic criticism suggests plainly that only the foolish crowd, ignorant of the law, would be tricked by one such as Jesus.

At this tense moment Nicodemus returns. The narrator tells us with excruciating ambiguity that Nicodemus "was one of them" (7:50). Which "them" are we to imagine Nicodemus as "one of": the Pharisees or the cursed crowd? It is a moment of truth for Nicodemus. He avoided Jesus' questions with silence, perhaps to think it all over, to pray about it, to speak with others among his peers who might dare to be open to Jesus. But now, with the official manhunt under way, there is no longer time for quiet reflection. Dare we hope that he will speak up and shout, "I, Nicodemus, a fellow Pharisee and ruler—I have believed in him!" Such a confession by Nicodemus and those like him might have changed the course of history and kept the Jesus movement within the tradition-bearing community of which Nicodemus was a part.

But instead of offering personal witness, Nicodemus appeals to due process: "Our law does not judge a person if it has not heard from him first and known what he is doing, does it?" Like many liberals in the United States who seek the securance of rights for the accused under the Constitution and its institutions, Nicodemus expresses his faith in the status quo. More important, he keeps his personal views aside, attempting merely to appeal to the religious system to which he shares allegiance with Jesus' accusers. In so doing, he sidesteps the invitation to be born *anōthen*. The risk is just too great.

Perhaps surprisingly to Nicodemus, but not to readers of the gospel, the prosecutors turn to bad-mouthing the attempt to appeal simply to the law's own procedures. They are revealed not to be loyal at heart to the Torah but instead to be about pure power politics. In this internal forum they, unlike Nicodemus, are willing to show what they stand for, despite the veneer of religious tradition that they use as a shield before the ignorant masses. They accuse Nicodemus of being "out of Galilee," the equivalent of calling him a country bumpkin, or more pejoratively, as our culture might express it, "white trash." Is he or isn't he one of their own? Once more Nicodemus is reduced to a pregnant silence. He can make confession for neither side. Like many of his time or ours, Nicodemus would like to have his cake and eat it too: to believe in Jesus privately without paying the required public price.

For the early Christian communities such an effort amounted to the worst sort of betrayal. As we will see at the end of John 9, the gospel's harshest criticism is leveled against those who in their heart know the truth about Jesus but are afraid of facing the consequences of witnessing to that truth. For communities or prophetic individuals under persecution, a single friend in high places can mean the difference between life and death. Nicodemus could have been just such a friend for many Christians. But, the gospel tells us, he remained silent, allowing the persecution to continue. The Judean ruler will have yet another chance, but not before Jesus has been executed and seems to all to be safely dead.

—PREACHING AND REFLECTION IDEAS—

Preaching Themes

1. Imagine where a character like Nicodemus might be found in our own setting; for example, a politician secretly sympathetic to an activist cause but concerned with reelection and loss of fund-raising sources; a professional comfortable with the wealth and success of his or her position but privately critical of organizational policy or practice; a church minister or leader supportive of "new" teachings (such as women's ordination or support for gays/lesbians) but concerned with loss of institutional authority and status. Consider how the community could support the "coming out" of such persons rather than leaving them in private fear of rejection and loss.

2. Consider human resistance to change and newness. Who are persons in our world, whether public or private, who offer ideas that seem to bear truth but imply difficult personal consequences?

3. Reflect on so-called liberal and radical approaches to problem solving. How can we discern when a system can be changed from within to provide justice in its sphere of influence, and when we are called to dismantle a system in favor of the birth of something totally new?

Small Group Activities

1. Imagine a present-day context for Jesus' encounter with Nicodemus and act it out with the group. Encourage the ac-

tors to ad lib as they imagine their characters might if allowed to speak more than the gospel presents. Spend some time as a group reflecting on both the experience of the actors and of those observing the drama.

2. Take some quiet time to get in touch with the Nicodemus in each one of us: What do we believe is "not possible" that at the same time appears to be God's call for us? What might God be calling us to allow to die in our lives so that we can be born again/from above? Invite those who wish to share their reflections.

3. Brainstorm among the group about some social problems that face the context in which the group lives, for example, homelessness and poverty, racism, environmental degradation, and so forth. Choose a particular issue for consideration. Brainstorm for ten or fifteen minutes to determine a wide range of possible steps toward solving the problem, writing them all down so all can see. Which of these steps are more like Nicodemus's appeal to the inherent justice of a particular social system, and which are more like Jesus' appeal to start from scratch?

Reflection Questions

1. *Personal:* What aspects of my lifestyle do I protect from the consequences that might flow from speaking openly about the gospel (such as physical security, financial wealth, social acceptance)?

2. *Social and cultural:* How does my culture—both locally and nationally—respond to criticism of "the system"? How do the consequences faced by dissenters differ in our culture as compared with other parts of the world?

3. *Ecclesial:* Is the church more like Nicodemus or like Jesus? What might the Christian community be called by God to allow to die in order to see or enter the reign of God?

4

The First Scrutiny

"Not to Be Born of the Will of a Man"

John 4:3-42

Once Jesus' (and the narrator's?) speech to Nicodemus is completed, Jesus begins a circuit around Judea gathering disciples. The gospel pauses in its reporting on Jesus to provide a second occasion to emphasize Jesus' superiority over John (3:25-31). Jesus is the "bridegroom," while John is the "friend of the bridegroom," whose cultural role was to establish the legitimacy of the marriage through his witness to its consummation. The wedding imagery recalled from the Cana episode will play a behind-the-scenes function in the encounter about to unfold at the well in Samaria.

In the meantime, Jesus retreats to Galilee to avoid a confrontation with the Pharisees over apparently competing community-building efforts (4:1-3). Rather than succumb to the worldly temptation of receiving human "glory" as the most honorable and powerful teacher, it is "necessary" for Jesus to begin the process of breaking down the doors established by the Judean power elite that block entrance to the reign of God. He must make the journey back to Galilee through "unclean" territory: Samaria.

The story of Jesus' encounter with the woman at the well in Samaria is one of the richest passages in the gospel, susceptible to numerous interpretations. Its multivalent symbols, grounded in a mixture of biblical and natural traditions, have generated an immense amount of thought, prayer, and conversation. But when considered within the overall context of John's gospel and with an ear toward its power as the first Lenten scrutiny reading, the narrative exemplifies the struggle over one of the Prologue's central themes: to be born "not of the will of a man."

During the thrice-annual pilgrimage that Galilean Jews would make to Jerusalem, an old feud would be confronted. On the west bank of the Jordan, between Galilee and Judea, lay the hated land of Samaria. For readers not familiar with this ancient antipathy, the narrator expressly tells us in verse 9 that "Judeans have no dealings with Samaritans." More specifically, this probably refers to the prohibition against sharing utensils, such as drinking cups, for fear of contracting ritual impurity. Behind this wall lay hundreds of years of hostility, the kind of hatred that, like Protestants and Catholics in Northern Ireland, can only come from religious differences combined with a shared (in part) heritage. To feel the depth of what Jesus does in Samaria, it is worth reviewing the history of the split between Judeans and Samaritans.

In 722 B.C.E. Assyria conquered Israel, the northern kingdom of the united monarchy of Israel and Judah. This conquest separated the two kingdoms for the first time in some two hundred years since they had first been united under King David. As described in 2 Kings 17:24-41, the Assyrian king, following common practice among empires, replaced the inhabitants of Samaria (up until then a portion of Israel) with people from other nations in order to diffuse the possibility of rebellion. The religious result was a number of hybrid customs mixing worship of Israel's God with worship of many national gods, including the practice of child sacrifice. As the biblical summary concludes: "These nations worshiped the Lord, but also served carved images; to this day their children and their children's children continue to do as their ancestors did."

The Babylonians conquered the southern kingdom of Judah in 587 B.C.E. Cyrus of Persia converted the resulting exile into colonialization some fifty years later. The population of Samaria had become, according to the book of Ezra, "the adversaries of Judah and Benjamin" (Ezr 4:1). The returned exiles had determined at this point to set about the task of rebuilding the Jerusalem Temple, which had been destroyed by the Babylonians. The mixed nationality Samaritans asked to participate in this rebuilding, claiming, "we worship your God as you do, and we have been sacrificing to him ever since the days of King Esar-haddon of Assyria who brought us here" (Ezr 4:2). However, the Judeans rebuffed this attempt at religious solidarity, finding the history of what they saw as idolatry too defiling to allow participation in the sacred rituals of national rebirth involved in Temple reconstruction.

The rejected Samaritans, in a "sour grapes" pattern too sadly familiar, responded by writing to the Persian king, warning that allowing Judah to rebuild the Temple would rekindle the rebellious nationalism for which Judah had become famous. Although the Samaritan epistle was temporarily effective in withdrawing Persian consent for the project, the stubborn Judeans set about the rebuilding program without approval, appealing to the previous permission granted by Cyrus. This ploy was effective and the Temple was rebuilt, but not without cementing the thick wall of hatred between Jerusalem and Samaria.

By the first century this hostility meant that pilgrimaging Judeans would sometimes cross the Jordan to "the other side" in order to go *around* Samaria rather than take the obvious route between Galilee and Jerusalem. This was the history into which it was "necessary" for Jesus to enter on his own way from Judea to Galilee. What Temple worship had separated Jesus would reconcile, but in a manner completely unimaginable to his disciples.

Jesus comes to rest in Sychar, a place mentioned only in John 4:5 in the entire Bible. Immediately, we are asked to associate it with powerful symbols: the field Jacob gave his son Joseph (Gn 48:22) and Jacob's "well." Jesus, "having labored on the journey, was sitting on the well." It is the sixth hour, midday, when the heat and light are at their peak.

Into this scene comes a woman of Samaria, to draw water. The gospel previously spoke of drawing what was expected to be water at Cana, when Jesus ordered the servants to draw the wine from the purification jars (2:6). The link with the Cana story will be reinforced by the detail in 4:28 that, upon returning to the city to report what she had heard, the woman left her water jar behind.

By the fact of her arrival at the well at midday, we already suspect she is an outcast. The well in a culture without indoor plumbing or a river or lake at hand is a center of social activity at morning and evening. In the cool of the day, the women gather at the well to share stories, complaints, and hopes for the day or night. This woman, though, comes alone during the heat of the day. We are led to wonder what it is that causes her to come to the well at this unsociable hour.

Before we hear another detail about her, Jesus has addressed her, asking simply and directly for a drink. Apart from the Jewish/Samaritan question, this opening of conversation by a man with an unknown woman was a serious violation of the cultural code. In a public setting it was rare for men and women to speak to one another apart from the necessities of the marketplace. For people of different clans and even different cities, this inclination toward noninteraction was even stronger. For foreign men and women even more of a presumption against discourse existed. For a *Jewish man* and a *Samaritan woman* to speak together was wholly unthinkable! Jesus, with no apparent regard whatsoever for this powerfully ingrained code, initiates a dialogue with her.

To Greeks and other non-Jews beginning the Lenten walk toward Easter, Jesus' initiation of the conversation with the Samaritan woman provides a powerful affirmation of their own invitation to dialogue with the Christian community. Furthermore, it underscores the often unasked-for nature of God's inbreaking into our lives. Just as we are busy going about our daily business, here comes Jesus with a proposal to overturn our lives altogether!

The incipient conversation is interrupted by a comic parenthetical comment about the disciples' alternative journey into the city to buy food. While the disciples participate in the established system of things (the marketplace), Jesus initiates new systems by breaking down the cultural systems that limit the opportunities for sharing of resources among people. The disciples' absence will leave them completely ignorant of Jesus' purpose in Samaria until after they have returned with the groceries in verse 27.

The woman expresses her shock at his unthinkable behavior. But Jesus moves the conversation from the "earthly" level of thirst and ethnic hatred to the "heavenly" level of the "gift of God," the question of his own identity, and the metaphor of living water. Further, he reverses the direction of the thirst-quenching; from asking her for a "drink," he challenges her to ask him.

Her response in verses 11-12 is complex. She starts out in the same vein as Nicodemus, interpreting Jesus' metaphor at the "earthly" level. But she quickly adds a second question that underscores the nationalistic implications of the location of the encounter. At the heart of the exchange is her ironic questioning of whether this strange Judean is greater than the Samaritan patriarch, Jacob. As with many ethnically marginalized peoples, she is quick to claim her identity in the face of a challenger from the dominant culture.

She may be an outcast woman drawing water at midday, but she is *still* a descendant of Jacob and *still* entitled to share in the limited but plentiful bounty of her inheritance. Judean men may see themselves as superior to Samaritan women, but he's certainly not superior to Jacob, her "main man"!

Jesus ignores her questions and continues about his own mission, the offering of the gift of God. Jesus twice uses "heavenly" language about the eternal value of the water that he gives. Further, the imagery suggests that not only will his water provide ultimate satisfaction, but it will overflow like a fountain, affecting those around the one who has received it.

In powerful contrast with the teacher of Israel who apparently gave up on Jesus at a similar point in the conversation, this Samaritan woman keeps the conversation going. Although she still thinks on an earthly level about being relieved of the exhausting daily task of coming to the well and quenching her bothersome thirst, she does in verse 15 what Jesus invited her to do back in verse 10: "Sir, give me this water."

From the quenching of thirst Jesus dramatically switches topics: "Go and call for your husband [Greek, *andra*] and come here." The woman responds to Jesus' command with the bare admission, "I have no husband." Jesus strips away further layers of this woman's vulnerability with his surprising awareness of her situation. We often hear this passage interpreted in terms of marital infidelity. However, as we saw in the Cana story, weddings and marriage are ancient metaphors for relationship with God, and we are more likely to be in tune with the text by pursuing this line of interpretation in the immediate case.

Why does Jesus ask the woman to call her husband to this place? How does he know about her personal life? An excerpt from Jeremiah may provide a clue:

> Thus says the Lord:
> I remember the devotion of your youth,
> your love as a bride,
> how you followed me in the wilderness . . .
> O house of Jacob, and all the families of the house
>   of Israel, thus says the Lord:
> What wrong did your ancestors find in me
> that they went far from me,
> and went after worthless things,
> and became worthless themselves? . . .
> Those who handle the law did not know me
> the rulers transgressed against me
> the prophets prophesied by Baal. . . .
> Has a nation changed its gods
> even though they are no gods? . . .
> my people have committed two evils:
> they have forsaken me,
> the fountain of living water
> and dug out cisterns for themselves,
> cracked cisterns that can hold no water.
>   (Jeremiah 2:2, 4-5, 8, 11, 13)

The "house of Jacob" has acted like an unfaithful wife by practicing idolatry, forsaking God, the true "husband" and "fountain of living water." What might this prophetic poetry have to say about Jesus' conversation with the Samaritan woman? Recalling the passage from 2 Kings 17 establishing the antipathy between Samaria and Israel, we find that exactly *five nations* are listed as infecting worship of God with worship of gods (2 Kgs 17:30-31). If we begin to see this anonymous woman of Samaria as the representative of her people, just as Nicodemus was a representative of a group, we find the relationship between her "husbands" and her current "man" to be an expression of Samaria's colonial past and present. If the five previous husbands are symbolic of Samaria's intermarriage with foreign peoples and the acceptance thereby of their false gods, her current man can be seen as *Rome*, with whom she "lives" but has not married. The Jewish historian Josephus in his book *The Jewish War* notes that the Samaritans did not intermarry with the Romans as they had with the previous peoples. In this context the woman's response in 4:19, "Sir, I see you are a prophet," and her statement about the place of worship are not a change of topic to avoid further questioning of her personal life but rather a direct acceptance of Jesus' statement of her national history.

The remainder of her response shows how clearly *she* understands Jesus' statement about her "men" as implying the question of nationality and religious loyalty. By introducing the question of "this mountain" versus "Jerusalem," the woman evokes a major point of contention in the history of Samaritan-Judean relations. A complex set of biblical and extra-biblical traditions link Mt. Gerazim through Jacob with proper—and improper—worship. Throughout the conflicting traditions runs one predominant theme: "our" ancestors established a place of religious worship, and upon this tradition, our *national* identity is grounded. The woman's question puts Jesus to the test: resolve this dispute once and for all, Mr. Prophet from Judea: which nation, Samaria or Judea, is the true descendent (and inheritor) of Jacob?

Jesus' answer, as we have come to expect, goes beyond her either/or nationalistic-religious vision and opens up unforeseen territory for her consideration: "Believe me, woman, the hour is coming when neither on this mountain nor in Jerusalem will you people worship the Father!"

In contrast with the "coming hour," when worship will take place on holy mountains, is the *present* hour, when "true worshipers will worship the Father in spirit and truth, for these are the ones the Father is seeking to worship him." The end of nationalistic worship may be an eschatological dream, but the community of Jesus' disciples exists *now*!

As Jesus insisted to Nicodemus that he and his people could not see the hoped for reign of God without being reborn in water and spirit, so he tells the Samaritan woman and her people: "God is spirit, and those worshiping that one must worship in spirit and truth."

The woman neither affirms nor denies Jesus' declaration but instead probes his credentials. By having her express the expectation of a coming messiah the woman's statement can be read as an indirect way of asking: are you really the one to replace our father Jacob?

Jesus' reply, after all the metaphorical speech, is surprisingly direct: "I am [Greek, *egō eimi*], the one speaking to you." It is the only time in John's gospel where Jesus expressly acknowledges the title messiah, Christ. He does so in the form of the first of many *egō eimi* statements that link his being with that of the one revealed to Moses at the burning bush (Ex 3:14). And it comes not to the Judeans who will eventually (and murderously) press Jesus for just such a confession (10:24), but to the Samaritans, and to a woman!

It is the latter social boundary that concerns Jesus' newly returned disciples in verse 27; they are so flabbergasted to find their rabbi speaking with a woman that they cannot speak. The silence of the disciples, filled in ironically by the narrator, leads readers suddenly to see them as outsiders in relation to the Samaritan woman, who has engaged Jesus in deep and meaningful conversation. Whereas the woman is perfectly willing to ask her "foolish" questions and thus expose herself to Jesus' potential criticism, the disciples do not dare to challenge Jesus' shocking intergender discourse, preferring their ignorance and "honor" in the sight of this foreign woman to the risk of growth in knowledge in the sight of the Messiah.

The woman apparently takes advantage of the new arrivals to leave her water jar and to share the news of the mysterious encounter with her kinsfolk.

Her announcement to the people follows directly from her messianic experience of being told "all things." Without another word the people respond to her call and begin the trip back to the well to find Jesus himself.

As they approach, we are returned by our omnipresent narrator to the well, where Jesus and his disciples are gathered. With their minds on their initial mission to go into the city to buy food, they offer some to Jesus in the impertinent form of a command. The previous conversation over thirst and water is modulated to the key of hunger and food, as Jesus for the first time offers his gathered disciples the sort of mysterious double entendre he has already given to the Judeans at the Temple, Nicodemus, and the Samaritan woman. He phrases it in verse 32 in terms of their ignorance, just as he did with Nicodemus (3:8, 10) and the woman (4:10). Again, afraid to embarrass themselves with an open acknowledgment of their ignorance (of which, ironically, Jesus is well aware), they speak to one another.

At the heart of their misguided internal questioning is one of the key theological premises of John's gospel: *Jesus' own disciples do not really know or understand him any better than do "outsiders."* Despite their initial enthusiasm replete with powerful titles—none of which Jesus affirmed—the disciples must stumble along in the dark just like everyone else. How difficult it is to learn to think (and act) like Jesus! One can make the commitment to baptism without fully understanding what the path of discipleship will entail. For the church in our own time, we proclaim Jesus' greatness but wish he would "eat" the food we provide from our systems of doctrine and dogma. Fortunately, Jesus ignores his disciples' attempt to mold him to their expectations and continues about doing the will of the One who sent him into the world.

With this context in mind, Jesus offers a parable. The emphasis is on words of *sight*: "Look, lift up your eyes, see the fields white for harvest!" If the disciples were to "lift up their eyes," they would see the Samaritans coming toward Jesus from the "field" provided by Jacob for his descendants. The next sentence anticipates Jesus' sending of his disciples on their own "fruitful" mission (15:1-8). He tells them that the one harvesting is already "gathering together" the fruit into eternal life, thereby "receiving" the reward, so that sower and reaper may rejoice together. These images are familiar eschatological symbols from the prophets (e.g. Is 27:12; Am 9:13). The Isaian prophecy expects the reconciliation of Samaritan and Judean, but the gospel gives it a special twist by expressing its fulfillment in terms of a new "synagogue" (from the Greek, meaning "to gather together"): the community of disciples, wherein those gathered will rejoice together.

Jesus then sends his disciples to harvest that on which they have not labored. We recall the narrator's description of Jesus' initial state at the beginning of the story as "having labored." But he then goes on to express it in plural terms in verse 38: "Others have labored, and you have entered into their labor." Jesus' parable makes clear that his unknowing disciples are being sent to participate in an ongoing mission, which has as its object the gathering together of true worshipers for the Father.

After Jesus finishes his parable, the narrator returns us to the observation of the arriving Samaritans, but only after adding a crucial detail: the people from the city are not only coming to check Jesus out, they have *already* believed in him because of the "word of the woman bearing witness." This outcast foreign woman has joined the privileged circle to which only John the Baptist belongs, those who have "witnessed" to Jesus. Although the first disciples responded by following and calling others, only this Samaritan has been described in this special way. As John has expressed his "word" to his people, so the woman has also done to her own. In effect, the anonymous woman of Samaria is the first Johannine apostle: one "sent" to share the good news. The harvest has already begun!

The response of the arriving Samaritans in verse 40 is fitting both for Johannine community members and for descendants of Abraham: "Therefore, the Samaritans came to him, asking him to remain with them, and he remained there two days." Their offer is both one of hospitality to the stranger and of acceptance of him as the Messiah. It is precisely what the Prologue told us Jesus did *not* receive among "his own" (1:11).

Because of Jesus' "remaining," we discover that "many more believed because of his word." What they have discovered is that this One is not only the messiah who supplants their father Jacob, but the "savior of the world."

The term *savior* was a common one in the first century for a revered person such as a philosopher or other leader, but *the full title "savior of the world" was one used exclusively for the Roman emperor.* The title is used of Jesus only one other time in the entire New Testament, also in the Johannine literature (1 Jn 4:14). Its meaning in 4:42 can be only that the Samaritans have come to see that Jesus is the One to replace for them the man with whom they also live who is not their "man."

With this reminder of the marriage imagery seen earlier in verses 16-18, the entire story is revealed to be shaped on a common biblical "type-scene": the well-courtship story. The concept of a type-scene is one familiar to us all: the detective "whodunit" where the least suspected person is revealed to be the killer; the western where the white people are the good guys and the Indians the savages. It is familiarity with such a western type-scene that allows for the success of a film like *Dances with Wolves*, where the expected stereotype is reversed.

Such basic story patterns were common in the Bible as well as within modern fiction genres. The Pentateuch contains three examples of the basic well-courtship plot: a man comes to a well, finds a maiden there, asks her for a drink, they converse, she runs home to tell her people what has happened, they return with her to the well and approve of the man, he returns to their home and marries the maiden. This is roughly how Isaac met Rebekah, Jacob met Rachel, and Moses met Zipporah (Gn 24:10-61, 29:1-20; Ex 2:15b-21). Jesus, however, meets not a maiden but a five-times-married woman! Rather than looking for another husband, our Samaritan woman is just looking for relief. And rather than looking for a wife, Jesus is looking for "worshipers in spirit and truth." The net result, though, is similar to the marriage celebrated at Cana: the messianic joy of God's presence brings back the "bride" whom Jeremiah had lamented for going after false gods. Jesus the bridegroom has bonded himself to the people "lost in the land of Assyria," forming a unity that "remains" far longer than two days.

The story of the Samaritan woman and her people encountering the savior of the world is thus seen as the dramatization of one of the central oppositions in the prologue: to be not born of the "will of a man [*andros*] but out of God." The Samaritans had previously found their identity, their birth, in the will of *men*: their ancestor Jacob and his well, the Assyrian king who mixed many nationalities in the conquered land of Israel that they occupied, the oppressor-Caesars with whom they lived but were not intermarried. They had struggled to maintain their sense of social self by claiming earthly fathers and a fatherland that inevitably pitted them against the neighbors with whom they fought for survival. By receiving Jesus and believing in him, they were reborn by the will of God. As the Nicodemus story reflected the failures of birth from the will of flesh and the unaccepted invitation to be reborn of spirit, this story reveals the possibility of rebirth that transcends nationality and racial identity. In the presence of the true savior of the world, one no longer needs to rely on one's fatherland to provide knowledge of who one is supposed to be.

In sum, the first scrutiny reading alerts Christians to a central conflict generated by confession of faith in Jesus. Despite centuries of wars grounded in Christian nationalism and imperialism, the gospel's perspective is that these concepts are really oxymorons. Similarly, the religious right's rhetoric about the United States as a "Christian nation" betrays a failure to take seriously the gospel call to put aside differences of ethnicity and nationality that interfere with the unity of the children of God. Perhaps such a choice may seem unrealistic in our world, where chaplains have blessed Senate and war machinery from the beginning. But the early Christians did not think it unrealistic, as they refused military service in the Roman empire. And later disciples, such as St. Francis and St. Ignatius Loyola, understood clearly that the Christian is a person without a country, save that of the realm of God. Just as "living water" does not respect human boundaries but flows wherever it wills, so too are disciples of Jesus called to be free of ethnic and national boundaries. The church's home is not in Rome, but wherever the "harvest" of true worshipers is waiting to be gathered in.

—Preaching and Reflection Ideas—

Preaching Themes

1. Consider the "Samaritans" in our world; for example, "communists," Iraqis and other middle Easterners, inner city African Americans. Where in our world might we be called to journey to encounter the "other" whose faith may provide something we need?

2. Reflect on the role of water in generating or resisting social intercourse. Consider particular bodies of water in your region that mark off territory and create competition for drinking, agriculture, or industrial uses. Consider how these boundaries might be broken down and the social consequences of making the attempt.

3. Reflect on the idea of fatherhood: what does it mean to be "born of the will of a man"? Consider how national or other institutional leaders (corporate officials, school sports coaches,

church leaders) instill loyalty by appeal to common stories grounded in "the founding fathers."

4. Reflect on nationalism as a form of idolatry. Help distinguish healthy loyalty and commitment to a social group (such as a church, a country, an ethnic group) from blind obedience that prevents the recognition of God acting in new ways.

5. Consider the commitment to baptism as a rejection of the ultimacy of patriotism. Use historical examples of times the church as a whole or particular holy individuals have stood against national authorities on the basis of their baptism (e.g., Acts 5:28-29). What current issues might put Christians in conflict with the will of national leaders?

Small Group Activities

1. Role-play the story, either in its biblical setting or in some situation in today's world, whether that of the group or some other. Allow freedom of imagination to fill in gaps in the story with the actors' own words. Highlight the role of the disciples "offstage" trying to figure out what Jesus is about. Spend some time reflecting on the experience of the role-play, both as participants and as observers.

2. Brainstorm to create a list of groups who make up "Samaritans" in our culture. Consider the means by which interaction between "us" and "them" is limited, for example, language barriers, differences in social and geographic location, stereotypes reinforced by the media. Discuss how those barriers might be broken down in simple ways.

3. Take quiet time to reflect on the personal struggle between commitment to God and commitment to nation, church, or other social or cultural institution that defines us. Invite those who wish to share a specific situation in which their loyalty to a worldly reality came in conflict with their faith commitment. Consider the *feelings* involved in such situations.

Reflection Questions

1. *Personal:* How do I experience my relationship between commitment to God and commitment to nation, church, or other

social institutions? Do they always fit together or do they sometimes come into conflict? How do I respond if I experience such conflict?

2. *Social and cultural:* What are the consequences in our society for refusing to provide absolute commitment to national loyalty? Name some people who have resisted the demands of the state in the name of their faith. Do we support or oppose such resistance?

3. *Ecclesial:* What has been the church's *historical* relationship with governments and other worldly institutions? Where in today's world *does* or *should* the church stand against nations because of the gospel? What are the consequences to the church?

5

The Second Scrutiny

To Be Born "Not of the Will of Flesh"*

TWO JOURNEYS BETWEEN GALILEE AND JERUSALEM: PREPARING TO HEAL BLINDNESS

The second scrutiny reading is the story of the healing of the person born blind in John 9. While this passage bears much literary and theological power standing on its own, its full meaning for the church is best understood when read in the larger context of the gospel. This involves following Jesus on his double circuit between Galilee and Jerusalem.

Jesus' encounters with Nicodemus and the Samaritan woman were, in a sense, private conversations. Although the people of Sychar and the discipleship community witness the conclusion of the latter episode, Jesus has largely practiced his ministry away from the crowds. Except for his bold inaugural denunciation of the Temple system in John 2, Jesus has avoided the scrutiny of official Judea and its supporters. In a parallel way, Christians on their journey of discipleship may find the experience of being or becoming part of a church community a relatively safe one, involving challenging ideas perhaps but mostly supportive relationships.

---

*This is part 2 of this theme. Part 1 was covered in chapter 3, "To Be Born from God: John 2:23-3:21," above.

For both the Johannine Jesus and his would-be followers, this protected period comes to an abrupt end once the world's powers get a whiff of the subversive nature of the gospel. Between John 4 and John 9, Jesus will lead his disciples and those who consider becoming such to an understanding of the way things are, a way diametrically opposed to what they have been taught since childhood. In essence, he teaches them about their "blindness" and then invites them to be healed and to learn to see.

The initial period comes to a conclusion at the end of John 4 with the healing of the son of a royal official in Cana of Galilee. Although suspicious of "signs and wonders" faith (4:48), Jesus announces the healing, which leads the entire royal household to faith. The juxtaposition of this story with that of the coming to faith of the Samaritans teaches that the community of Jesus' followers allows for no class distinctions: both ethnic outcasts and the privileged elite are welcomed.

Reversing the Betrayal of the Covenant (John 5)

Following this scene Jesus returns to Jerusalem. The terrible price of the royal city's failure to live according to the covenant is laid out before his and our eyes: "a multitude of the sick, blind, lame and withered" are gathered in the shadow of the Temple, like heat-grate sleepers in the shadow of the White House—or an urban American cathedral. No commentary from the narrator is necessary to express the sense of betrayal revealed by this pathetic scene.

Jesus finds an individual among the multitude who is described as having been waiting at the pool for assistance in healing for thirty-eight years (5:3). Jesus' simple command to "rise, pick up your mat and walk" leads to a confrontation between the healed one and the Judeans because of the violation of Sabbath incurred in the carrying of the mat. Rather than protect the identity of the healer from the hostile questioners, the healed one "names names." As a result, the persecution of Jesus begins. Even worse, when Jesus attempts to justify his behavior as an imitation of what he sees his Father doing, the persecution turns murderous. Jesus' ultimate sin in the minds of the Judeans is "making himself equal to God" by "calling God his own Father" (5:18).

It would not be hard for later disciples to see their own experience in this cause for persecution. As we recall, the Prologue invitation to become "children of God" calls disciples into the identical relationship with God of which Jesus is accused by the Judeans. The period of protection for Jesus comes to a sudden and violent end with the healing by the pool at Bethzatha. In the same way, once word is out that his followers claim the Fatherhood of God over the fatherhood of Abraham, the anger of the Judeans will burst forth against the discipleship community, too.

In this context we can read the speech Jesus makes in John 5 as a model for the disciples' own defense in the face of accusations of "calling God Father." Jesus' statement follows the classic biblical courtroom procedure of calling witnesses to the accused's honorable status in the community. In the ancient world a trial was not so much about facts as about character. The charges against Jesus (and subsequently, against his followers) suggest that he claims honor not rightfully his. The witnesses he calls on his behalf (the Father, John the Baptist, his own works, and the scriptures) testify to the justice of Jesus' testimony about his relationship with God.

Again following traditional courtroom procedure, Jesus concludes his defense with an attack on his accusers. Not only are they wrong about *his* relationship with God, they are also wrong about their own. They are accused of a lack of faith in Moses and an absence of the love of God. They are empty shells, devoid of covenant fidelity, bent on destruction of what they do not understand, of what threatens their worldly power.

Jesus' speech prepares would-be Christians for the hostility which they may face from their peers. As we have seen, the baptismal commitment requires a stance in witness against the world's hypocrisy and injustice, one which speaks openly on behalf of a gospel unaligned with institutional power arrangements. Jesus' claim puts him outside the Judean religious system, because it expresses his faith in a God immediately available, not one who requires mediation through a priestly establishment. In the early churches this was understood by many as a rejection of official Judaism, which indeed it was. However, it was not a rejection of Jews or of Judaism as a whole. Rather, it was a claim that the religious system's supporters were themselves the betrayers, those who had traded the "glory from God" for the "glory from one another" (5:44, cf. 12:43).

For now, Jesus' charges go unanswered by the Judeans. He has apparently taken them by surprise with his bold challenge to their authority and sincerity. They will be better prepared, though, upon Jesus' return to Jerusalem in John 7. At Tabernacles, Jesus and the Judeans will go head to head in a battle of enormous proportions. But first, Jesus must clarify for his would-be followers just what it means to be the Messiah.

Challenging Messianic Expectations (John 6)

John 6 places Jesus in the role of a new Moses, the very one, he has just told the Judeans, who will accuse them of infidelity to the covenant. The narrator creates an atmosphere redolent of exodus and covenant: Jesus upon a mountain on the other side of the sea of Galilee at Passover. A hungry crowd is gathered in the wilderness, looking for a sign from God that the messiah has truly come into the world. And a sign is given to them: the provision of bread and fish until all were filled.

The Galilean crowd would certainly have included large numbers of disaffected peasants, those considered "cursed" by the Pharisees in Judea for their ignorance of Torah (7:49). However, what the Pharisees meant by ignorance was not lack of familiarity with the ancestral stories passed on from generation to generation. Rather, it was the peasants' ignorance of the Pharisaic *interpretation* that led them to be seen by the elite as cursed.

It is a distinction common in most religious and political systems between what anthropologists sometimes call "the great tradition" and "the little tradition." The former is the institutional, official religion promoted by the elite, largely for the purpose of maintaining their own social power and prestige. The latter is the unorganized collection of stories and rituals told and practiced by ordinary people when the officials aren't looking. The history of both Israel's and Christianity's faith reveals how this twin trajectory has always bifurcated the tradition. For example, even during the heady days of Israel's monarchy centuries before Jesus, tribal peasants in Galilee largely ignored or even rejected the claims of religious (and political) authority from

Jerusalem in the south. The story of the rebellion against Solomon's son and the attempt by the rebels' appointed king to prevent the annual pilgrimages to Jerusalem testifies to the vying for power between the great and little traditions (1 Kgs 12).

Thus, the crowd following Jesus across the sea to the other side is expressing its collective desire to offer allegiance to a different religious leadership. The fact that these people are in the wilderness at Passover rather than where the official religion expected them to be—in Jerusalem—reveals their lack of loyalty to the Judean status quo. When Jesus provides bread, many would surely recall Moses' words about the meaning of God's provision of manna in the desert (Dt 8:2-3).

Their understanding of the wilderness feeding as bearing messianic implications is expressed by the crowd's acclamation, "This is truly the prophet, the One coming into the world." Their statement announces their belief that a word from God to Moses in Deuteronomy has finally been fulfilled: "I will raise up for them a prophet like you from among their own people; I will put my words in the mouth of the prophet, who shall speak to them everything that I command" (Dt 18:18).

Jesus, unwilling to be "made a king" by the crowd (6:15), withdraws from them. His messiahship is different from that of Israel's popularly anointed monarchs, whose role it was to lead the people as a warrior in battle against ethnic enemies (cf. 2 Sm 2:4; 5:3). Jesus' reign does not depend on popular approval. In fact, his next mission is to reveal to his followers just what a fickle and superficial measure of success popular approval is.

In place of the symbols of popular kingship, Jesus offers his disciples the symbols of the Creator. Jesus' walk upon the stormy sea conjures up images of God's primal battle against the forces of chaos and darkness, recalled in the psalms (Ps 107:25, 29-30).

The psalm's storm-calming imagery is placed in the context of people lost in the wilderness through their own sinfulness, brought into desperate straits that only God can transform into safety. The battle is bigger than the wilderness crowd imagines. They look for a warrior who can provide a military victory over the Romans; Jesus offers instead the presence of the one God, whose enemy is chaos, sin, evil.

Jesus' words to the disciples express for the first time to them his identification with the hidden name of God, the *egō eimi* of the burning bush (Ex 3:14). We may recall that the disciples who now hear this awesome self-identification of their master were off buying food when he announced it to the woman of Samaria (4:26). Now, after Jesus has expressly rebuked their second effort at marketplace economics (6:5-7), they hear it for themselves.

The watery walk and Jesus' response provide assurance for potential disciples that Jesus is who he will claim to be at Tabernacles during his war of words with the Judeans. The church, too, will be called to take up Jesus' battle against darkness, empowered by the presence of *egō eimi* in their midst.

But the crowd did not witness this revelation. They come the next day, chasing after their would-be king. Jesus immediately goes to work to refute their sign-faith, inviting them into a less spectacular but ultimately more powerful form of relationship. The "work of God" to which the Christian community is called is not to engage in violent revolution but to "trust in the one sent forth" from God (6:29).

The subsequent exchange between Jesus and the crowd is filled with irony. The core of the issue is the meaning of *bread*. As we have seen, the manna provided by God in the original Exodus was, as interpreted by Moses (as interpreted by the author of Deuteronomy, writing after the militaristic monarchy had collapsed into Babylonian exile), for the purpose of teaching people *not* to rely on bread alone. Instead, the people are counseled to put their trust in God's word. Jesus calls upon this tradition to subvert the crowd's messianic expectations, basing his case on Deuteronomy. National security as a strategy failed Israel the first time. Furthermore, the crowd's nostalgic yearning for a military messiah reveals the people's desire to revert to the system of sacred violence, which the Jerusalem Temple had translated from the human sacrifice involved in war-making into animal sacrifice. By refusing to attend the cultic rituals in Judea and chasing after Jesus in Galilee, the crowd has shown its clear rejection of Jerusalem's form of worship. Can the people be born anew into a human family that rejects scapegoating violence altogether, or can they only imagine a return to the old, failed dreams of Israelite empire? Jesus warns the crowd not to go backward.

Jesus offers an alternative: the security of life in covenant community. For Christians listening to John's gospel late in the first century and beyond, this meant living in *eucharistic* community.

In the terribly graphic words of John's Jesus, "Unless you munch the flesh of the Human One [much more graphic in Greek than the Pauline or synoptics 'eat my body'] and drink his blood, you have no life in you. . . . The one munching my flesh and drinking my blood is remaining in me, and I in that one" (6:54, 56). The body of the self-sacrificing One (e.g., 10:17-18) takes the place of both animal and enemy victims at the center of the new community's worship.

By the time Jesus gets to this shocking climax of his exposition of the scriptural paraphrase "He gave them bread from heaven to eat" (6:31), the crowd has turned hostile. This transformation is expressed in John's gospel through the use of the term *Judeans* to refer to Jesus' opponents, beginning in 6:41. Although Galilean Jews, the crowd reveals its underlying acceptance of the Judean ideology, despite its rejection of the Judean collaboration with Rome, which maintains the oppression. The people continue to want a messiah who will liberate them from the foreign empire and restore Israel's political freedom. This mind-set was one common to first-century Palestine, and took many forms. From the guerrilla warfare that plagued Judean officials up through the destruction of Jerusalem to the hope for holy war that motivated the Qumran covenanters, most Jews who sought social transformation put their trust in this sort of messiah. In a word, the gospel sees them all as *Judeans*.

The implications of accepting Jesus' alternative messiahship are well understood by his audience. Even his disciples call it a "hard word" (6:60). The difficulty lies not so much in the acceptance of the equation, Jesus' flesh=God's bread, but in the social consequences of participating in a eucharistic community amid imperial supervision. When one untangles the layers of metaphor in Jesus' word, one finds a ground level that is to be taken both literally and metaphorically.

The mystery of eucharist challenges believers physically to eat a substance that appears to be bread but is understood within the faith community to be truly Jesus' flesh. And therein lies the rub: to "munch my flesh" means to participate in the celebration of eucharist within an outcast community, one subject to both Judean and Roman persecution. This interpretation, of course, depends on a vantage point late in the first century, that is, the time of John's gospel. Eucharist is the second sacramental "gate" through which Christians were called to go. Baptism—the rebirth in water and spirit that Nicodemus could not accept—initially identifies one with the Christian community. Once performed, it is completed, never to be performed again. But eucharist invites regular celebration, repeated public identification with the discipleship community. For people living in a village culture, a person's movements would be easily noticed and recorded in the communal memory. Jesus' "hard word" challenges those who would follow him to make their commitment to him and to his community known regularly to all who witness.

So what was the risk of such an identification? Why does the hard word cause some of his disciples to return to their previously rejected lives (6:66)? The answer lies in the socially marginalized location of the early churches. Whereas Jews, especially before the fall of Jerusalem, could claim a national history for their religion, Christians had no such support. The "liberality" of imperial Rome allowed most colonial nations to practice their native traditions, so long as that practice allowed for the paying of taxes and the offering of incense to Caesar. Many pious Jews resisted the obvious idolatry implicit in offering incense. But because Rome had made advantageous political alliances with Jewish client kings such as Herod, such resistance was largely ignored. Christians, though, had no such political arrangements to provide leeway for their religious resistance. They were a people without a "man," without a king to defend them against their enemies. From Rome's point of view, they were *atheists*. This was the primary charge with which Rome justified its persecution. In one of the great ironies of history, participating in regular eucharistic celebrations verified the accusation that the Christians were people without a god.

Historians tell us that Rome rarely sought to persecute Christians directly. But when confessing Christians were turned in to the authorities as resisters to the deification of Caesar, Rome responded harshly. Thus, John 6 comes to a close with Jesus' warning to the disciples who remain with him that their community is not a safe place: one of them is "a devil" (6:70).

The Messiah Comes to the Temple at Tabernacles (John 7–8)

One of the clearest places in John's gospel where the narrator highlights the contrast between Galilee and Judea is at the beginning of John 7. Jesus, we are told, intends for the moment to avoid "walking" in Judea because the "Judeans were seeking to kill him." His "brothers" urge him back to the capital for the sake of gaining publicity for the cause. It is unclear whether they are sincerely supportive of Jesus' mission but misapprehend its method, or whether they are cynical critics of what they believe to be Jesus' own desire to make a name for himself. In either case Jesus identifies their challenge to him as originating with "the world" in which the brothers' own loyalty lies. After refusing to be coerced into following their reading of the "time," he proceeds to return to Judea anyway, but in secret.

The occasion is the feast of Tabernacles. The visit to Jerusalem finds the crowd "murmuring" about him, trying to decide among themselves if he is "good" or whether he "is misleading the crowd" (7:12). But for fear of the Judeans, all of this conversation takes place in hushed tones. It is up to Jesus to break the silence in the boldest possible ways. First, he goes directly to the Temple and begins teaching all who dare to be seen listening. A series of arguments unfolds in which all the Judean "conventional wisdom," which denies the possibility of Jesus' sort of messiahship, is voiced by those gathered for the feast. This leads the chief priests and Pharisees to send out the police to capture him.

Jesus, unafraid of arrest, stands up at the most sacred moment of the liturgical celebration and loudly subverts the Judean ideology. To appreciate the power of Jesus' actions and words and their effect on the world view of the disciples, we will benefit from taking a step back to consider the nature of the feast of Tabernacles.

Tabernacles was one of the three main feasts of ancient Jerusalem that required pilgrimage to the Holy City (the others being Passover and Weeks, also known as Pentecost). All three were adopted from eastern neighbors of Israel and originated as agricultural festivals. As the traditions developed, each became associated with a particular aspect of the movement from Egypt to the Promised Land: Passover with the Exodus itself, Weeks with the Torah, and Tabernacles with the period in the wilderness.

Tabernacles, in its agricultural aspect, was a joyous fall festival celebrating the grape and olive harvests. As such, it was accompanied by the drinking of new wine and dancing. It became identified with the "booths" or "tents" used as temporary shelters in the desert, as described in Deuteronomy 16:13. This also matched the harvest practice, when temporary workers lived in similar shelters in the fields.

By the post-exilic period the feast became associated with the end times, the *eschaton*. Zechariah 14, a reading on the first day of the festival, envisions all nations going up to Jerusalem with "no rain upon them" (14:17). Prayers for rain were likely a part of the fall festival, to bring on the season following the hot summer and provide water for the coming months. The image of "no rain" anticipates the end of time, when there would be no worry for the next season.

The feast was celebrated with an enormous amount of liturgical pomp and circumstance. One of the primary festivities involved the daily priestly procession from the pool of Siloam to the Temple altar, where a golden flagon of water was poured out in memory of God providing water from the rock struck by Moses in the desert.

The second festivity of significance to John's gospel was the light ceremony, in which four golden candlesticks were set up in the Court of the Women in the Temple. Atop each candlestick were golden bowls filled with oil, in which wicks made from the garments of the priests floated. The light from this event shined throughout the city, as a symbol of God's presence in the Temple, and by extension, in Judea.

The gospel finds Jesus "on the last great day of the feast" crying out, "If anyone is thirsty, let them come to me and drink!" (7:37) It is hard to imagine the shock and scandal of such an act and claim. It is as if someone stood up in St. Peter's in Rome on Easter morning and shouted, "If anyone wants new life, let them come to me!" With this statement Jesus publicly repudiates the entire Temple ideology. And in a complex reference to scripture which is taken up at his death, he continues by claiming that the true "living water" comes from the heart of people, not from a self-aggrandizing religious establishment.

Once again he is proclaimed by some as the Prophet, while others go further and name him messiah (Christ). But there remains further division among the crowd, which is not yet ready to let go of what it has been taught about the expectation of a Davidic warrior-messiah.

After the narrator returns us to the inner workings of the Sanhedrin amid this public furor (see "Nicodemus's Challenge to Be Born *Anōthen*," p. 27 above), Jesus speaks again. This time, he takes down the other symbolic pillar of the Tabernacles tradition by claiming to be "the light of the world." This leads to successive trial-like encounters, first with the Pharisees, and then with a more mysterious group, "the Judeans who had believed in him" (8:31). The thrust of both confrontations is the issue of who speaks with authority from God. This takes the form of an argument over *paternity*; whom can each side rightfully claim as "father"?

By the time the exchange is completed, mutual death threats have been hurled. The Judeans, after accusing Jesus of being possessed by a demon and being a Samaritan (he doesn't deny the latter charges), pick up stones to kill him because of his claim "before Abraham came to be, I AM [*egō eimi*]" (8:48, 59). Standing within the Temple precincts, the stones with which they threaten to murder their victim can only be the building blocks of the Temple itself. The mob violence that would destroy Jesus will also cause the dilapidation of the Temple (cf. 10:31-33). Jesus, on the other hand, accuses them of being "liars" and "murderers" like their father the devil, and tells them that they will "die in their sins" (8:44, 24).

What can the effect of all this be on Jesus' disciples? Are they even around to witness the verbal battle? We have heard nothing from them at Tabernacles. It is Jesus' moment to speak "openly" when no one else will. The crowd murmurs, the Sanhedrin conspires secretly, and perhaps the disciples are off hiding, watching from a distance without taking sides publicly.

We must assume that they have at least heard of the debate and its world-overturning rhetoric from the Teacher. All those whom the disciples have been taught represent the presence of the sacred in the world—according to Judean ideology—have been unmasked as devil-worshipers. The Temple, in which generations of their ancestors celebrated God's triumphant presence, has been challenged at its core. The crowd—excited, confused, frightened—has been put in crisis. Either Jesus is good and therefore speaks the truth about himself and about the Judeans, or he is a misleader of the masses, in which case the Judeans are biblically correct to attempt to stone him (Dt 13:6-11). Can the bold wonderworker from Galilee truly be the messiah? If so, then the entire official religious system must be rejected. If Jesus speaks and does the truth, then everything the people have been taught by their religious leaders has been revealed to be grounded in the Big Lie. It is this terrifying, world-shattering possibility that leads us directly into the second scrutiny, wherein Jesus both reveals and heals blindness.

HEALING AND REVEALING BLINDNESS (JOHN 9)

The fourth Sunday of Lent features the reading from John 9 of the person born blind and his trial in the court of the Pharisees. It is a reading structured as a drama in seven discrete scenes, arranged in chiastic fashion. Although it is impossible to know whether this passage was actually performed dramatically within the early Christian communities, such an effort fruitfully reveals the power of the story today. Whether in a living room small group setting or before a large congregation, acting out the confrontation between one learning to see and those becoming increasingly blind brings out the emotional elements of the narrative that mere reading can obscure.

In effect, the story is the inverse of the Nicodemus story. The following table shows some of the contrasts:

	Nicodemus	Person Born Blind
social status	ruler of the Judeans (elite)	"unclean" beggar (outcast)
named	yes	no
time setting	night	day
source of encounter with Jesus	comes to Jesus	Jesus comes to him (twice)
response to Jesus' invitation	unbelieving questions	obedient action
response to Pharisees' derision	silence	bold speech
relationship with Judean ethos	obedience	excommunication

We can see from these contrasts that the story in John 9 models for the church what it means to accept Jesus' invitation to be born "of water and spirit," that is, to be born "from God" by being baptized into the discipleship community. During the course of the sequence of encounters, the person born blind learns to see the "world" the way it really is. In the course of that learning experience, his eyes are opened to who it is that has touched him, and what the consequences are of remaining true to this newfound vision.

More than perhaps any other episode in John's gospel, the second scrutiny passage benefits from careful and close reading. We will look at each scene individually, paying attention to the small textual details that can make a big difference in how we interpret both the story and the call to discipleship.

Jesus and the Disciples: Questioning the Causes of Sin (John 9:1-5)

As we have seen, the story opens directly upon Jesus' hasty departure from the Jerusalem Temple, where the Judeans were attempting to execute him in accordance with their understanding of the Torah. The narrator provides no change of scene, either in terms of time or location. Although the common lectionary begins the reading as if it was sharply delineated from the preceding narrative, the story's power is revealed by recognizing the continuity between its events and those at Tabernacles in John 7–8.

Jesus has rhetorically undermined the legitimacy of the Temple and publicly dishonored the Judeans, who rally to its defense by trying to dishonor him. He has boldly shown no fear of worldly threats, trusting in the one he calls by the intimate name Father. He has revealed for all who observe his unprecedented acts the falsity and violence of the religious establishment and those who support it.

What can the effect of all this be on his disciples? What is the effect of it on *us*? Is the gospel's critique of Judean hypocrisy limited to the long-gone circumstances of first-century Palestine, or do Jesus' criticisms remain true today in our church and world? For the passage to speak to the struggle of Christians living after the destruction of the Temple to trust in Jesus, it has to be read more broadly than the bounds of its historical context.

For both the disciples in the story and those throughout the ages, Jesus' demolition of the "divine canopy" providing the aura of sanctity to the world's unholy alliances continues to challenge. For centuries it threatened to subvert the legitimacy of the Holy

Roman Empire, which sought to justify its imperialism and plunder under the cover of Christian legitimation. It threatens in our own time all propagandists who would justify an oppressive and violent status quo as being divinely sanctioned, whether explicitly or implicitly. Certainly, the "holy" language of the United States' founding documents and subsequent theopatriotic rhetoric falls within the scope of Jesus' harsh criticism. Jesus turns our world upside down, revealing those in positions of respected authority often to be "liars" and "murderers," while those reviled by the elite are often the ones most able to see God's truth.

Recognizing and accepting this reversal is perhaps the most difficult aspect of discipleship. For those in positions of power—like Nicodemus—it is virtually unimaginable. It is equally difficult for the poor and marginalized, but for different reasons. They have been taught the official perspective for so long that it is very hard for them to be persuaded that the leaders are liars. Both in the world of the gospels and in our time, movements directed at helping the poor to recognize their oppression and rise up in rebellion have been extremely difficult to organize and sustain. In the gospels we see the crowds turning against Jesus when the defenders of the status quo express their strong opposition. Even within the discipleship community we see Jesus again and again frustrated over his followers' refusal to let go of the "conventional wisdom." And as we know, the revolution of the proletariat has been largely a Marxist fantasy, as a bit of today's bread in the hand seems more real than the promise of a future feast. Dostoevsky's Grand Inquisitor episode in *The Brothers Karamazov* is one of the best fictional portrayals of this reality.

It is in this context that Jesus and his disciples encounter one "blind from birth" (9:1). A close look at the Greek text reveals that the encounter is meant to be considered more broadly than that between Jesus and an individual blind beggar. The literal meaning is "person blind from birth." That is, there is no *a* or *the* limiting the blindness. Although the subsequent narrative is dramatized through the literary vehicle of a single individual, the central issue of the story is that of *humanity* blind from birth. This is the situation that evokes the disciples' question: "Rabbi, who sinned, this one or this one's parents, to be born blind?"

Without this universal perspective, the question's premise is nonsensical. Can the disciples really be suggesting the possibility of *in utero* sinfulness? From the wider viewpoint, though, their query makes perfect sense. In the context of Jesus' world-over-turning actions, the disciples have come to recognize that *they* are blind beggars on the roadside. Those they thought bore God's authority have been revealed to be the worst sort of criminals. The institutions whose golden gleam reflected God's light to Is-rael are gilded cages, imprisoning the people in a web of lies. They ask, how did this happen? Whose fault is it that we can't see things the way they are? Is it our parents' fault or our own? Put in later theological language: is the problem original sin? Or from another angle: is the etiology nature or nurture? Or still another: is it social sin or personal sin that must be healed?

These kinds of questions engender heated dialogue among many people in our world. We yearn to solve the riddle of evil. We engage endlessly in either/or arguments under the illusion that our war of words is leading us somewhere. To the disciples and to us, Jesus responds clearly: stop asking useless questions and get about the business of healing! He denies the premise of their inquiry: that "sin" is the cause of blindness. In the conclu-sion to the story Jesus will explicitly reverse the assumption by claiming that "sin" is found in "seeing" but failing to respond to the truth of what one has seen (9:41). Rather than seeking to cast blame, the disciples are directed to the more difficult task: revealing the works of God (9:3).

Repeating his Tabernacles proclamation, Jesus tells his disciples, "I am the light of the world" (8:12, 9:5). He will now reveal this to the disciples by shining that light in the darkness and not al-lowing that light to be overpowered (1:5).

Accepting the Invitation to Be Born from Water and Spirit (John 9:6-7)

The description of Jesus' healing actions is filled with reveal-ing detail. The first act is to "spit on the ground," a behavior which itself would get Jesus into legal and social trouble. As a matter of Torah regulation, bodily fluids were expected to re-main inside the body, at the risk of incurring ritual "impurity" for an improperly placed discharge. In particular, spitting was (and often still is) seen as an unclean public act.

Jesus joins spittle with soil and forms clay, which he puts upon the eyes of the blind one. The acts are richly symbolic, evoking texts both from earlier in the gospel and from much further back in biblical memory. At Tabernacles, when Jesus proclaimed himself the answer to thirst, he and the narrator combined to develop a link between water and spirit that now comes into play. Jesus spoke of "living water" that flows from the "core" (literally, "womb") of a person (7:38). In the next verse the narrator explained this as a reference to "the spirit that those trusting in him were about to receive." Thus, we have the equation, "living water from the core" = "the spirit." In John 9 Jesus' saliva incarnates "living water." Therefore, we find Jesus' instruments of healing to be spirit and soil, precisely the elements used by God to create human beings in the first place (Gn 2:7). What God did for the first humans, Jesus does for those invited into the Christian community. In other words, the act of healing blindness involves a *call to be reborn* not of "the will of the flesh" but "of God."

What might this experience be like from the perspective of the one born blind? Unlike the blind beggars of the synoptic gospels, who loudly cry out to Jesus for healing (Mk 10:46-48; Lk 18:35-40), the gospel of John narrates an unasked-for encounter. It reveals a God whose grace comes like a slap in the face, startling its recipients into response. Although the life of a blind beggar was certainly a harsh one lived out at the bottom of the social pyramid, first-century Palestine was not a world with dreams of upward mobility. One born blind would be unlikely to have the slightest expectation of a life change, other than for the worse. Positioned on the outskirts of the Temple, the blind beggar would be in direct sight of those pilgrimaging to Jerusalem for the thrice-annual feasts. As an adult who had lived with his disability since day one, he had learned to accept and to deal with his fate. The invitation to wash that he receives after the placing of the clay on his seemingly dead eyes might well come as an unwanted intrusion, one which challenges him to give up his accustomed practice and begin life again.

We are given the name of the pool as Siloam, which the narrator tells us means "having been sent forth." We may recall that the pool was the source for the Tabernacles water ritual, which Jesus has already subverted. He has transformed the pool from a tool of the status quo to an instrument of healing, an act in the restoration of covenant fidelity.

We should note that Jesus' command to the one born blind to wash at the pool contains no promise of healing. Yet the man wordlessly obeys. The narrator announces the healing in the most low-key way imaginable at the end of 9:7. This style emphasizes the focal point of the story, which is not so much on Jesus—who now disappears from the stage—but on the call to discipleship of one now, for the first time, able to see.

Witnessing to the Neighbors and Pharisees (John 9:8-17)

From the moment the gift of sight is noticed, it generates controversy. The journey of the healed one from blindness to sight creates a crisis first among the neighbors and others who have known the person only as a beggar. *Their* eyes are confronted with a situation for which both their experience and their theology have left them unprepared. The neighbors presumably know of his blindness from birth, while the others have seen him begging near the Temple. Their exchange is directed among themselves. They do not deem the beggar worthy of a role in the conversation. As often happens, people gossip about the unusual experiences of their neighbors rather than inquiring directly. One thing is clear: the beggar's bowl has been abandoned.

Despite being talked *about* rather than *to*, the healed one speaks up anyway, with the simple yet profound words, "I am" (*egō eimi*). His affirmation of his identity uses the same words claimed elsewhere in the gospel only by Jesus as Jesus' self-identification with God. The first testimony from the newly reborn appears to claim quite a bit!

His intervention into the conversation leads them to turn the inquiry directly to him. Their first question is the usual one for those challenging unexpected experience: "how?" It echoes Nicodemus's own twice-asked "how" question to Jesus (3:4, 9). The response is clean and straightforward: "The person called Jesus made clay and anointed my eyes and said to me 'go to Siloam and wash.' I went, therefore, and washed and I saw."

The answer reveals much about the character of the former beggar. First, although Jesus did not name himself to the man, his name is known. The man may have been blind, but he wasn't deaf! Second, he is either ignorant or unconcerned about what will momentarily be revealed to readers to have been a Torah violation: the making of clay on the Sabbath. One way or another, he has not accepted the dominant ideology's claim to authority. Third, he interprets what the narrator called simply a "putting" of clay as an "anointing." He is already beginning to understand his healer as one with authority from God, in contrast with his apparent rejection of the authority of Torah. The Greek word for the act of anointing, *epichrio*, is one brought to center stage for the Lenten scrutinies, as catechumens are anointed with oil and chrism on their journey to baptism and confirmation. The healed one's act of interpretation is honored in memory by all those who are invited to follow the path which the gospel lays out in this story.

The response leads to the second question to the healed one, this time about the whereabouts of Jesus. But the man will not testify to matters of which he has no knowledge. Once this interrogation begins, it moves under its own steam. The questioners take the person now described as "the one once-blind" to the Pharisees. The reason for this movement is noted in verse 14: it is the Sabbath, a day on which clay-making is prohibited. Whether the first questioners are motivated by obedience to the Torah or simply curiosity at the anticipated response of the self-appointed guardians of Torah, we are not told. The effect is the same, however. The confrontation between sight and blindness has begun.

When the Pharisees take their turn at the question of "how," the answer is amended. No longer is the healer named. No longer is the act described as an anointing. Absent is the reference to Siloam. It is clear that the once-blind one understands, even if he does not seem to accept, the Sabbath violation issue that is in the air. He therefore protects Jesus as best he can while remaining true to the core of his experience. His refusal to "name names" before the authorities is in direct contrast with the behavior of the person healed on the Sabbath earlier in the story, where the issue of ongoing sin was also in the air (5:14-15).

As with the first group of inquisitors, the response of the once-blind one leads to a crisis among the Pharisees. They are divided over two logically inconsistent consequences of their religious system. Premise A: people from God keep the Sabbath. Premise B: sinners cannot perform signs such as healing the blind. A crack has opened in their divine canopy! How will they resolve this problem? Will they admit the human-made nature of their dogma and adjust it to fit the ever-newness of God's powerful creativity? Or will they insist on their system's authority and deny the data? This conundrum is precisely the one with which any authorities claiming the absolute nature of their ideological systems are faced when facts intrude.

But before they determine their tactics, they dare to ask the once-blind one for his opinion. And in his now characteristic style he answers, "He is prophet." Again, there is no *a* or *the* qualifying the response. It seems to be the gospel's way of suggesting that the one who has been healed of blindness finds in Jesus the embodiment of the prophetic spirit, perhaps the Awaited One anticipated by Deuteronomy 18:15. As the challenge of witnessing to truth deepens, so does the newly born disciple's sense of the authority of his healer.

The Parents' Fear of the Judeans (John 9:18-23)

In 9:18 the scene suddenly shifts and one set of characters is replaced by another. Gone are both the Pharisees and the healed one; in their place are the Judeans and the one born blind's parents. The scene about to unfold is the chiastic center of the passage. Why has John's gospel placed this particular encounter at the peak moment in the drama?

With the entrance of the Judeans, we notice that the circle of inquisitors has become steadily wider. First we found the immediate group of neighbors and passersby, those whose direct experience was at issue in their questioning of the cause of the apparent healing. Next the interrogators became a more abstract group, the Pharisees, whose interpretation of Torah and social status accompanying that interpretative stance was implicitly challenged by the Sabbath clay-making. Now we have the group that, in Johannine symbolism, has the broadest interest at stake. Those whose lack of faith is on the line are all those who identify with the dominant culture of Judea: religious leaders, Jerusalem merchants, craftspeople, money changers, and any others whose economic and social security relies on the maintenance of the status quo. In other words, it is the "world" that now takes its turn questioning what has happened.

The Judeans bypass the one born blind, however, to question his *parents*. We may recall that parents were one of the blindness-causing options in the minds of Jesus' disciples at the beginning of the story (9:2). Jesus' answer to the disciples cleared the parents of the charge of having sinned in a way that caused their child to be born blind. But that does not mean that the gospel sees them as innocent!

Parents are a rare phenomenon in the Christian scriptures. We find many references to fathers and mothers, either singly or as a pair, but few to the combined unit. Their presence in our passage focuses our attention on the nature of one's birth. Previously, the healed one had been challenged to testify to his identity as "the one who used to sit and beg" (9:8), to the cause of his healing (9:10, 15), and to the identity of his healer (9:17). Now the parents are given a two-part question: Was he really born blind? If so, how can he see now? The question is at the heart of the call of the baptized to witness to their rebirth. And yet, here it comes not to the one whose new sight is at issue but to those who have provided the earthly birth of the potential disciple.

Thus, the gospel puts in dramatic form Jesus' aphorism found in the synoptic gospels: "Brother will betray brother to death, and a father his child" (e.g., Mt 10:21). The acceptance of Jesus' invitation to be born again/from above will entail too powerful a shift in social geography for disciples to expect public support from their parents' generation. The parents will be willing to testify to the blindness of their children from birth—a blindness the parents, ironically, share—but not to the cause of their offspring's new insight, which threatens the safety not only of the children but of the parents as well. It is an ancient form of what was called in the 1960s "the generation gap." The gospel warns would-be Christians that those claiming to see in a world of the blind will be ridiculed by some, persecuted by others, and ultimately cast out of "polite" company. And throughout this process of becoming marginalized, support will not likely be found from those whose security depends on being accepted within the mainstream.

The parents in John's gospel act out precisely this scenario. Their witness is as narrowly stated as possible, as they explicitly encourage the Judeans to put the hard questions to their son. The narrator makes equally explicit the reason for their willingness to throw their child to the wolves: their fear of being ostracized by their community. How many parents in our own time have faced the difficult task of answering to others about the "inappropriate" behavior of their progeny? Our culture has learned to accept the symptoms of adolescent rebellion without blaming the parents, so long as it remains "just a phase." But when one makes serious commitments that fly in the face of "all that we taught you," the refrain "it's your life—we're not responsible for your choices" can often be heard. Each of the gospels, in its own way, cautions us to be prepared for this sort of backhanded "gift" of personal freedom.

The specific cause of the parents' fear is being associated with "confessing him as the messiah." It seems clear that this concern arose from the time of the Johannine community rather than from the time of Jesus. For at least one generation after Easter, followers of Jesus apparently were not rejected automatically by the synagogue. The book of Acts portrays an early Christian community equally at home at Temple and eucharist. What we have in John's gospel is a narrative comment that clarifies the perspective of the story: the journey to discipleship after baptism had come to imply an absolute choice between old and new. The parents' refusal to support their child lies at the center of the second scrutiny to remind the church of the cost of naming and claiming one's religious experience. With that reminder, the focus turns once again to the one born from God.

Witnessing to "Them" a Second Time (John 9:24-34)

Just as quickly as the parents are ushered onto the stage, they disappear from the scene in 9:24. The Judeans have extracted from the parents an answer to the question of whether it is their son who was born blind, but not to the question of cause. However, as the interrogation continues, it is the identity of the inquisitors that is at issue. The narrator tells us that "*they* called for the person who was blind a second time." But which "they," the Judeans or the Pharisees? In the progression of the story, the one now healed is called to testify not before a specific group but before the ubiquitous "them." We all know this hostile group. It is the nameless, faceless opposition that evokes fear in the heart of anyone daring to think or act outside the bounds of propriety.

What will "they" think of me? What will "they" do to me? It is the most difficult opponent of all, because it is the one created by one's own inchoate fears.

"They" do not ask a question but rather challenge the healed one under oath to support the prevailing theological wisdom. They have solved for themselves the paradox of the Sabbath healing. Despite the testimony of the parents, the "miracle" must give way to the Law. Messianic actions *cannot* violate their interpretation of Torah; God must obey their ordering of reality. The upshot is that the healer must be a sinner. Agree with this, they demand, or face the consequences.

The first followers of Jesus found themselves confronted with a similar demand. In the process of testifying to their experience of Jesus as healer and teacher who washed them clean of their blindness, they came to see the blindness of those who claimed to speak for God. It is this experience to which the man witnesses during this scene as he refuses to engage them on their own terms. Rather than respond to the charge of "sin," he simply reiterates his experience.

Of course, such persistence is absolutely infuriating to defenders of the world's system of justice, then and now. They push once more for a specific answer, hoping to find a contradiction in the testimony that can raise a doubt about the credibility of the witness. The integrity of their system and of their own status is on the line. If Jesus and the one he healed are not repudiated, the entire Judean structure will be at risk. So it is in all courtrooms where people testify to divine experience outside the regulated channels of law or grace. They must be branded criminals for the system to survive. Claiming that God has acted in unapproved ways will regularly get one in trouble!

Rather than cower in the face of this vicious assault, though, the healed one gains strength. He understands the stakes and boldly turns the question back at the inquisitors. Ironically, in a story about blindness and sight, his challenge to them is in terms of *listening*. And to make crystal clear that he knows the goal of their deadly game, he twists their "logic" back around on them: "You don't also want to be his disciples, do you?"

With this challenge they drop the veneer of civility and turn to personal attack. The either/or they present is between "that one" and Moses. Once again, they express the absolute certainty of their understanding of how and when God speaks. With that, the healed one knows that there is no honorable way out. His opponents have painted themselves into a corner. The healed one is now quite pleased to make the case for the absurdity of their position. He has gone from blind beggar to expert lay theologian, not by virtue of rabbinical study but in the school of the courtroom. His alternative theory of the case is compelling and irrefutable. Fact: I was blind and now I can see. Fact: God listens to those who do God's will. Fact: From ancient times we have never heard of anyone opening the eyes of one born blind. Conclusion: If my healer (who is not named) were not from God, he could do nothing.

It is precisely this logic that led the Johannine community to its understanding of Jesus. And it is the inquisitors' response that led them to understand the cost of discipleship. To speak unauthorized truth to power calls for expulsion. Both "truths" cannot stand side by side.

Being Found on the Outside (John 9:35-38)

For followers of Jesus attempting no more forceful act than consistent, open, and truthful testimony about how God has acted in their lives, the experience of being thrown out of "civilized" society can be terribly painful. Gone are the security and comfort of old friends and family. Gone are the familiar places of home. If that were the end of the story, few would dare to risk washing in the pool that means "sent forth."

But John's gospel does not leave the excommunicated one alone. Jesus, who has been absent throughout the interrogation, hears about the expulsion and finds the would-be disciple. It is only now that the question of trust in the Human One is presented. It is a new inquiry; the healed one has not previously known of this identity of Jesus. But his openness to trust his healer is apparent, and the ritual of commitment is completed with a prayerful bow.

The process of coming to faith in Jesus presented in this story is the gospel's paradigm for the journey of discipleship. First comes the unasked for gift of grace, which includes within it the requirement of obedient response. Second comes the challenge from a darkened world that rejects a healing light it cannot control. Third comes a dual enlightenment that learns the truth about

Jesus at the same time it discovers the blindness of the world. Finally, there is the social crisis that necessitates the involuntary movement out of one world and the voluntary movement into a new one. It is this journey to which the church is called to recommit itself each year during Lent.

The Question of Sin Revisited (John 9:39-41)

The story of the second scrutiny reading is not yet complete, however. Jesus announces the paradoxical judgment the presence of the Light of the world brings: "that those not seeing may see and the ones seeing should become blind" (9:39). But before we can reflect on this paradox, another group of inquirers intervenes: "the Pharisees who were with him." Their question, paralleling that of the disciples at the beginning of the episode, asks not about the sinfulness of parents or children but about the issue of their own blindness.

Before we look at Jesus' answer, it is essential to understand who these inquirers are. They are certainly not the ones who have just expelled the healed one. Those Pharisees are on "the inside." Their business is done. Having rid themselves of the troublemaker whose experience disrupts the perfection of their systematic theology, they turn to their next order of business. These Pharisees are on the *outside* and are described with a simple but telling detail: they are "with him." In John's gospel to be "with" someone is to state one's allegiance. When Judas comes with the soldiers and police to arrest his former master, we are told that he was standing "with them" (18:5). And when Peter watches from a distance as Jesus is brought into the house of the high priest, the narrator tells us that Peter is "with" the high priest's servants, standing around the fire (18:18). In these two moments where loyalty under pressure is demanded, two disciples are found "with" others.

The Pharisees, in contrast, are "with" Jesus on the outside. With this recognition we can hear their question about blindness as one which seeks assurance that they are not in the same boat as those on the inside. *We* are with you, they claim. Surely we're not blind, are we?

Jesus' response cuts through their pretense. "If you were blind, you would have no sin. But as you are saying 'we see,' your sin remains." For John's gospel, the Pharisees on the inside are arrogant, blind guides, stumbling in the dark. But the gospel does not condemn them for this. Blindness from birth, after all, knows no other option. But for those who claim to be "with" Jesus, who claim to "see" the truth, protestations of ignorance are invalid.

What is the sin that Jesus tells them "remains"? Why does the gospel conclude the story with this harsh condemnation of people who seemingly are on Jesus' side of the schism? We have heard of such people before in the gospel. They are the ones who know that Jesus is a teacher sent from God but who cannot accept the challenge to be born again/from above. They are the ones so invested in their status as Pharisees that they cannot imagine God requiring that they give it all up to express their commitment to the covenant that their whole life situation is devoted to upholding. They are the Nicodemus Pharisees, the ones who would have their cake and eat it, too. The gospel casts its condemnation upon them precisely because it is their desire to remain Pharisees while claiming to "see" that leads to the persecution and excommunication of so many disciples who have "come out."

We in the United States are all too familiar with this dilemma. The church puts us to the test on sexual ethics and internal issues of church order but rarely calls its members to the either/or of worldly vs. divine glory. For the early churches this divide was clear. If the Nicodemuses would come forward and renounce their loyalty to the system of oppression that rewards them with status and success, the system would itself come crashing down. Their testimony on behalf of Jesus and his followers would both protect the disciples and break up an unjust system. But their refusal to leave their past behind supports the vicious status quo and leaves disciples dangling. The blind within the system can be understood and dealt with on their own terms. But the "seeing" Pharisees within the community of Jesus' followers are a bitter pill that the gospel refuses to swallow.

Those who have passed through this second Lenten gate have been warned about one of the most difficult consequences of discipleship. If it were not for the existence of the church "on the outside," it would be nearly impossible to accept. But there remains still another threat in the hands of the opponents of Jesus. If the risk of excommunication is not enough to deter discipleship, perhaps the threat of death will do it.

—PREACHING AND REFLECTION IDEAS—

Preaching Themes

1. Consider attitudes toward "sin." How much time do we spend as a church defining sin and sins, and how much do we spend working to remove the root causes of evil in our culture?

2. Reflect on the intrusive nature of grace and healing. Recall stories of persons known to the preacher and/or the congregation whose lives were going along fine until God "interrupted": the apostle Paul, St. Francis, the slave-owning author of the song "Amazing Grace," Dorothy Day, or less famous examples in the local community.

3. Consider the difficulty of witnessing to one's faith publicly. Often the most painful courtroom is the one in which our closest family, friends, neighbors and co-workers sit in judgment. Consider the church as a "safe house" for those rejected by "their own" because of their commitment to discipleship.

4. Reflect on the painful process of learning to see uncomfortable or embarrassing truths about the social world in which we live: our city or country, our people, our church. Consider how the biblical prophets such as Jonah and Jeremiah preceded the one born blind in feeling called by God, even against their own wills, to understand the sinfulness of the world around them.

Small Group Activities

1. Role-play the entire episode in one of several contexts: a) the world of John's gospel, b) the group's own world, or c) some other social situation in the modern world (for example, a third-world country or a different part of one's own city or region). Feel free to be imaginative with the "script." Take time afterward to reflect on the experience by sharing the feelings of playing a given character, watching other characters in action, or interacting with a character or characters.

2. Take some quiet time to reflect individually on the experience of being called to witness to one's faith: What did it feel like in

anticipation? What did it feel like in practice? How did people respond? Invite each person who wishes to share something of that experience.

3. Take some quiet time to consider individually one's own growth in "learning to see." What looks different about the world after whatever experience of discipleship you have had? What truths about yourself, the world around you, or about God have you discovered in the process of articulating your experience to others? Invite sharing of the experiences. Use candles as symbols of shining the light of each person into the space you are in.

Reflection Questions

1. *Personal:* How have I been called to witness to my faith experience to my neighbors, family, or other persons in my social world? What have I learned about myself, about my world, or about God in the process of articulating my experience?

2. *Social and cultural:* How does our culture respond to people who experience truth in ways not in harmony with the "conventional wisdom?" Who are people among us who have had this experience (for example, people of color in relation to European-Americans, immigrants, gays/lesbians, women in relation to men)?

3. *Ecclesial:* What truths do I see that might lead me into conflict with church authorities? Do I speak up? Why or why not? Where might I turn for support if I experience hostility or rejection in expressing my own truth?

6

The Third Scrutiny

"Not to Be Born of the Will of Blood"

John 11:1-53

FROM TABERNACLES TO CHANUKAH (JOHN 10)

The second scrutiny story ends with the condemnation of the "Nicodemus disciples" at the end of John 9, but Jesus continues to talk as if there were no break in the scene. Thus, in preparing to understand the third scrutiny, the story of Lazarus, we need to take a moment to follow the narrative as the previous scene continues in John 10.

The chapter marker was probably placed where it is (over a thousand years after the gospel was written) not because of a change of scene but because of the abrupt change in *metaphor* in Jesus' speech. He switches, without taking a breath, from blindness to sheep and shepherds. Jesus uses this new image as he continues to address the Pharisees "with him" who are unwilling to give up their pursuit of the world's glory. The imagery in 10:1-18 is thickly layered and can be confusing upon a first reading. But when we take the time to follow the text carefully, we see that the first theme with which Jesus challenges those sitting on the fence of Christian commitment is the identity and character of God's appointed shepherds. The Hebrew scriptures frequently use the shepherd image to refer to healthy community leadership (e.g., Nm 27:16-18), as well as to criticize those who lead the people astray (Jer 23:1-4; see also, Ez 34, Mi 3, Zec 10). In John's gospel, Jesus identifies himself with both aspects of this tradition. He is the successor to the first Joshua (translated into Greek as *Iēsous*, "Jesus") who saves the people from being without a shepherd and he is the one who replaces the evil shepherds who scatter God's flock. Those truly among Jesus' flock, he tells the Pharisees "with him," recognize the voice of the true shepherd, and will not follow "strangers."

The narrator tells us that none of this made sense to Jesus' audience (10:6). Just as Nicodemus could not understand Jesus' metaphor of birth from above/again and its call to give up prior loyalties in favor of baptismal commitment (3:3-9), neither can his compatriots now grasp the radical criticism of the Judean religious establishment of which they are a part.

Jesus continues with a somewhat different image, that of the door to the sheepfold. This time he broadens the attack to include not only the religious elite but also the revolutionary leaders who compete with the Christian community for the hearts and minds of the people. The two groups are referred to under the labels of thieves and robbers, respectively. Other leaders, he tells them, are in it for themselves, to garner wealth and worldly power. In dramatic contrast Jesus' leadership is self-sacrificing and unafraid of the "wolf" that threatens the flock. Who would you prefer as your shepherd? he asks, directing the question both to the Pharisees in the story and to would-be Christians over the centuries.

Finally, he notes the expansion of his own flock beyond those in "this fold" (10:16). As readers know, but the Pharisees with him may not, the Christian community will include people from all cultures and classes. As we heard during the first scrutiny reading, Jesus' followers are to be people with no respect for national boundaries and the idolatrous patriotism that often accompanies them. "Children of God" cannot also be children "of the will of a man." The Judean religious establishment dreams of all peoples processing to Zion (Jerusalem). Jesus, on the other hand, welcomes members to his flock without requiring a change in ethnic identity.

The scene ends in 10:17-18 with a statement that will come to the fore during the footwashing scene in John 13, the reading for Holy Thursday. For now, though, attention remains on the absolute nature of the sheep's choice from among the shepherds. For the Nicodemus Pharisees and their successors, Jesus has laid out the reasons for the extreme nature of the crisis in leadership that his presence in the world generates. Only he is a "good shepherd." Others—whether Jerusalem priests, latter day kings and presidents, or other institutional office holders—are "hired help" who, when push comes to shove, usually look out for their own self-interest. The gospel's hope is that when presented with this stark contrast the Judeans will turn away from the hired help and embrace the leadership of the good shepherd.

The response recorded in 10:19-21 is, as it was at the beginning of chapter 9, divided. Jesus' words seem to be those of someone possessed by a demon, yet the healing of a blind person remains the act of God's agent. The curtain falls with this "schism" (10:19) in the air.

The second half of John 10 takes place within the context of Chanukah, the feast commonly celebrated by Jews in our time in memory of the Maccabees' military victory over the Seleucid oppressors two centuries before Jesus. Among New Testament texts only John's gospel refers to it. It was a relatively recently developed feast, one which evoked fiercely patriotic feelings, especially in Jerusalem. Its memory certified the system of sacred violence at the root of Israel's nationalistic yearnings. Much of the messianic hope in the air at the time of Jesus was fueled by the celebration of the Maccabean "success" and the dream of its repetition.

Jesus is surrounded by Judeans as he walks boldly through the Temple, unafraid of his murderous opponents. With Temple stones in hand they await the words from his mouth that will liberate them to carry out their murderous plot. Rather than shrink from them, Jesus, like the healed man in the previous encounter, turns to sarcasm in ridiculing their hypocrisy (10:32). But their ears remain closed as he eludes their grasp once more at the end of the chapter.

It is the last direct confrontation between Jesus and the Judeans until the passion. He retreats across the Jordan to "the other side," to spend some time among friends and believers. And while in this place of safety, the call comes that one of his beloved back in Judea is sick to the point of death.

CONFRONTING THE FEAR OF DEATH (JOHN 11:1-53)

Of the various lectionary readings from John's gospel, the story of Lazarus is the one most likely to be misunderstood without consideration within the broader context of the gospel. In many ways it does seem to stand outside the plot of the complete gospel. Its characters and setting are previously unknown. Its internal plot seems on the surface to be far removed from the concerns that surround it within the narrative. But for a church struggling to discern its vocation in the world, only a reading that flows from the previous scrutinies makes sense out of its confrontation with human attitudes toward death.

The pattern of the story's structure should by now be familiar. Jesus first engages in conversation with his disciples, who misunderstand his mission and, by implication, their own. The disciples then disappear from the stage while Jesus encounters others and challenges them to a new stage in their own faith journeys. Finally, the reactions of observers are sorted out, some coming to faith and others remaining in the darkness of the world.

We have seen that the first two scrutinies invite Christians to take the risk of severing their previous commitments to the world and entrusting themselves to the community of Jesus' followers. The encounter in Samaria dramatized the challenge to be born "not of the will of a man" in accepting birth from God the Father rather than from national patriarchs. Those who take up this challenge become people without a country, outside the community of patriots. The second scrutiny illustrated the cost of being born "not of the will of the flesh" in rejecting the blindness required for acceptance into "the world." Those who learn to see and dare to witness to their new vision are cast out of the community of Judeans, that is, those dependent for their identity upon acceptance within a status quo built on lies, violence, and false honor.

But one further challenge awaits those who would be baptized into Jesus' discipleship community. The world's powers exert much influence by threatening dissenters with ostracism and excommunication. But for some, these threats are not enough to squelch subversive associations and behaviors. Ultimately, Jesus' opposition is not embodied in a particular institution or social order that can be overcome by simply walking away. The final enemy is the one Jesus knows is waiting in the wings to frighten away those who consider themselves his most loyal followers. The opponent to be overcome is the one that empires and other oppressors have used since time immemorial to maintain order: the threat of death.

Throughout this story we will see all the various attitudes human beings bring to their experience of the presence of death. Onto the stage of Bethany in Judea come all the darkest fears and internal doubts that threaten to undermine the commitment to follow Jesus wherever he might lead us. Only when the light of the world has shined into these dark recesses and has not been overcome will the church be empowered to witness boldly and without fear to the good news.

Setting the Stage: Rumors of Anointing for Death (John 11:1-4)

The curtain goes up in John 11 with the introduction of three new characters, the siblings Lazarus, Mary, and Martha, of the village of Bethany. Then, strangely, the narrator describes Mary as the one "who anointed the Lord with oil and dried his feet with her hair" (11:2). What is strange is that this episode will not be narrated until the next chapter! It is assumed that as we listen to the story in chapter 11 we have already heard the entire gospel before. The comment also has the effect of introducing the first reaction to death before anything about Lazarus's own perilous condition has been reported. That is, one possible response to impending death is *to help prepare the one about to die to walk the journey to the other side.* Having introduced this possibility, the narrator drops it for now. We will focus on this theme in more detail when we reach John 13.

For now, the text returns us to the issue at hand: the dire illness of Lazarus. Word of the crisis goes out from Bethany across the Jordan to where Jesus is on retreat among friends and followers. And from the other side we hear Jesus' response, announced to no one in particular, that "the glory of God"—not death—will have the last word.

The mysterious exchange of communication between the sisters and Jesus introduces another element of the unfolding drama. Jesus is on the other side precisely because of the death threats that abound in Judea. The sisters, apparently aware of the situation, send their message along the secret channels that underground communities have built up whenever and wherever such threats lurk. Whether the movements of slaves from South to North in nineteenth-century America, Central American refugees closer to our own time, or conspiracies to resist Nazi Germany's persecution of Jews and others, people determined to be free in the face of the shadow of death instinctively learn to keep their conversation close to the ground. Throughout this passage we will be reminded of the secrecy required to protect Jesus from Judean stones.

Walking While It Is Still Day (John 11:5-18)

One of the most troubling aspects of the story for many readers is Jesus' reaction to the message, as described in 11:6: "As he heard, therefore, that he was sick, he even remained where he was for two days." A superficial understanding of Jesus' motivation may perceive this as toying with death for the sake of performing a public miracle. It is as if Jesus were allowing a beloved friend to go through the pain of death so that Jesus could show off for the crowd. But as we have seen, Jesus is wholly uninterested in engendering faith based on "signs" (2:23-24, 4:48). His goal is not to prove his own power but to empower his followers to be willing to risk everything for the sake of love.

When he announces to his disciples the invitation to return to Judea, they make clear their understanding of the risk of such a journey. We should note how quickly they distance themselves from their master. Whereas Jesus speaks of "*us* going," they respond in terms of "*you* going" (11:7-8). They are amazed at Jesus' bold recklessness but are not about to include themselves in the plan. Their attitude illustrates the second option in the face of impending death threats: *avoid taking risks that might arouse the opposition.*

Jesus answers their query first in the familiar metaphor of day and night, light and dark. They are to be people of light, not those cowering in fear of the dark. Then he turns to a new image: sleep and death. Lazarus's illness, in Jesus' eyes, is not final. It produces "sleep" from which their friend can be awakened.

Once again the disciples' lack of understanding is portrayed with ironic humor. Jesus knows that Lazarus is in fact physically dead, but he can see past this barrier to the life that continues. The disciples, though, unable to stretch their imaginations this far, can only guess that Jesus' words suggest that Lazarus has not yet died. They urge leaving the situation alone, which, of course, would leave their master safely with them far from Judea. This uncovers the third attitude toward death that the story confronts: *denial.* How often we would like to dream that the cancer will go away, the fever recede, if we only wish it to be so! One must be careful here to distinguish fantasy from the authentic urge of people of faith to prayer, to the secure acknowledgment that an ill loved one is in the safe hands of the Creator. The disciples in the story, though, are not described as prayerful, as Jesus will be outside Lazarus's tomb. Rather, they are simply in denial, unable to come to acceptance of the reality of the situation. True prayer can only take place in the consciousness of reality, as well as reality can be perceived. The disciples, in contrast, substitute wishful thinking for prayerful acceptance.

When Jesus makes the situation known to them and renews the call to join him on the journey back to Judea, only Thomas can respond: "Let us go, too, so that we might die with him." How many possibilities lie in Thomas's simple sentence! Who is Thomas suggesting they accompany in death: Lazarus or Jesus? And is his attitude one of faithful commitment, sarcastic fatalism, or that of the brave soldier? Neither the narrator nor Jesus provides a clue to this previously unmentioned disciple's purpose in speaking so boldly. But when the narrator continues in 11:18, there is no mention of the disciples coming along for the trip. We will not hear from them again until the supper at the sisters' house in John 12.

Do You Believe? (John 11:18-32)

In keeping with the clandestine nature of Jesus' approach to Bethany, we must infer from the narrator's comment in 11:17 that Jesus has heard from one of the friends of the family that Lazarus is now four days dead. It is not until 11:30 that the narrator tells us that Jesus has waited in a place outside the village, away from the Judeans who have gathered around the mourning sisters at the house. Each sister's movement to Jesus is done in secret, based on word passed through protected channels of communication (11:20, 28). The scene is constructed with a double stage: one outside the village, and one at the house.

Physical movement in the story is a telling aspect of each character's commitment. In the opening scene we saw the struggle between Jesus and his disciples over going back to Judea, the place of death threats. In the middle section of the episode we find a range of movements: Jesus from the safety of "the other side" to the dangerous place outside the village; Martha and Mary from the house to where Jesus is; the Judeans from Jerusalem to Bethany. Each movement expresses the carrying of a particular world view into a new setting where it must respond to a new situation. This series of movements invites readers/listeners to consider what they carry from their own places of origin to new places, especially those where death is in the air. The central question becomes, how does each character's starting point prepare him or her for this encounter with death?

The first group we hear about is the Judeans. Throughout the gospel, as we have seen, *Judeans* stands for all those who depend upon and support the status quo in Judea, as defined by the Jerusalem elite. The fact that these Judeans are described as having come from the capital city suggests that they are other than simply family and village friends who help grieve the loss of a loved one. Rather, they are professional mourners. It was not uncommon at the time for people of means to hire people to wail with them during the aftermath of death. If this seems odd to us, we should stop to consider the economics of our own death marketplace. Musicians, caterers, florists, undertakers, limo drivers, and others earn a living helping perform the rituals of grieving in our culture. The mourners illustrate the fourth attitude toward death presented in the story: *treat it as an occasion for making a living.*

What the text alerts us to is not the inappropriateness of these Judean mourners at the family home but of their inherent resistance to Jesus. The Judean burial ethos (cf. 19:40) has filled the sisters' home with those who would cause further mourning in the house if they knew that Jesus was nearby. In order to receive the support of their beloved friend, the sisters must leave their own home to journey to a different safety zone.

Martha goes first, leaving Mary at the house to avoid arousing the Judeans' suspicion. Her opening statement to Jesus, echoed verbatim by Mary upon her own visit to Jesus, is poignantly ambiguous. It is both a simple expression of deep friendship and an inchoate hope for something more: "Lord, if you had been here, my brother would not have died." That both sisters use precisely the same phrase suggests that it is something they have discussed during the four days of waiting: "When the Lord gets here, this is what we'll say." It is a sentiment any of us might express at the delayed arrival of a loved one to the deathbed, knowing that the absent one's presence might have been enough to give the dying one strength to survive, if even for a bit longer. It expresses the fifth attitude toward death presented in the story: *the hope of preventing it from happening.*

But Martha takes this hope a step further by naming her trust that "whatever you might ask God, God will give you." We who have heard this story many times often take her cryptic statement as expressing a hope for resurrection. But would it be likely that Martha would realistically have dared to express such a radical hope? Nothing in her experience—or in ours, I presume—leads us to expect that it is possible for one four days dead to be brought back to life. The specification of "four days" indicates that Lazarus has been dead so long that his spirit would have departed from his body, around which it was commonly believed to hover for three days. And nothing in the Judean theology would have expected even the messiah to have such power. Only a previous statement by Jesus—which there is no reason to believe that Martha and Mary had heard—would serve as preparation for what was to come. When Jesus was defending himself against the Judean charges that he "made himself equal to God," he proclaimed that "the hour is coming and is here now, when the dead will hear the voice of the son of God and those having heard will live" (5:25; cf, 5:28-29).

The test of what Martha dares to hope for comes in the following verses. Jesus' apparent platitude, "Your brother will rise," is met with impatience. His statement is about as consoling as the common grave-side cliche, "Your loved one is with God." True enough, but what good does that do us, left alone on this side of the great divide? Her response emphasizes "the last day," a long time to wait to be rejoined with her brother! Can't Jesus do better than that?

At the center of the story, and perhaps at the center of the gospel, is Jesus' following statement. Without a clear and resoundingly affirmative answer to its accompanying question, the church is not ready to confront the powers of death in the world. And although many lifelong Christians easily mouth the right words, how many truly dare to believe the impossible dream proclaimed in Jesus' awesome sentence:

> I AM the resurrection and the life.
> Those believing in me, even though they die, will live.
> And everyone living and believing in me will never die at all.
> Do you believe this?

It is obvious that Jesus cannot expect his words to be taken literally. Even the most devout Christians have not escaped the shuffling off of this mortal coil. And yet, it cannot be "only" a metaphor, for metaphors will not get us past the fear of pain and loss that this story is intended to overcome. What message can Jesus be attempting to convey to Martha and to all who risk becoming followers of Jesus?

The first part expresses a Christian commonplace, which was, however, a radically new idea when first stated by Jesus. Over the centuries, it seems that it has been easier for Christians to believe that God is with them *after* death than it is to believe that God is here *during* this earthly life. Martha has expressed the prevailing Pharisaic theology, which itself was considered by conservatives like the Sadducees to be an unwarranted innovation, grounded in the apocalyptic vision of the prophet Daniel (e.g., Mk 12:18; Dn 12:13). Jesus radically revamps this concept, shifting from an eschatological hope to a present one. For believers, death is a transition that does not break the bond between lover and beloved. No "last day" appointment is needed.

For a faith community under persecution, this hope grounds the courage to walk into the jaws of death without becoming paralyzed by fear. It is the hope that has allowed martyrs throughout the ages to continue to speak the truth without heed to the threatened consequences. Jesus invites Martha, on behalf of the entire discipleship community, to be the first to respond to this promise.

The second part of Jesus' proclamation has to do with those still alive. That is, it is a promise not about afterlife but about the way in which a disciple is to walk through *this* life. Death is both a physical and a spiritual reality. The first part of Jesus' statement assures us that the experience of the former does not imply the experience of the latter. In the second part we are dealing with the possibility of spiritual death in this world. For John's gospel, those who are blind are also dead. More precisely, those who have not been "born of God" but have only received life from the alternatives rejected in the Prologue (1:11-13) are only physically alive. Their spiritual life has not yet come into being. Baptism and the practice of life in eucharistic community brings about this new life. For these people, Jesus announces, spiritual death is no longer possible, so long as one continues to trust in Jesus.

Martha's answer reveals a limitation that is still often present in the church. On the one hand, she responds, "yes, Lord!" If she had stopped there, things might have been fine. Instead, though, she continues by showering Jesus with a stream of potent titles. She has believed that Jesus is the messiah, and so on, but has she believed that he is "the resurrection and the life"? Similarly, the church has had no trouble proclaiming its faith in the Jesus of exalted names. But has it trusted that the world's death threats are impotent in the face of God's promises? For Martha, at least, the narrator keeps this issue open until the next scene.

Groaning in the Spirit (John 11:33-44)

Mary takes her turn at going out to visit Jesus, but despite Martha's attempt at secrecy, the Judeans follow. The entire scene is filled with weeping. Jesus responds to this weeping with an outpouring of emotion that is virtually untranslatable. The Greek words search to express a depth of feeling unprecedented in the gospel. The literal meaning of the first of the two Greek words suggests the snorting sound of an angry horse. Facile readings see this simply as Jesus' sadness at the death of Lazarus or his sympathy for his beloved friends. But this reading trivializes the text by ignoring the fact that Jesus has orchestrated the entire episode from the beginning. He purposefully remained in Galilee to allow Lazarus to die, so that "the glory of God" might be revealed. That the *Judeans'* response to Jesus' own tears is to link the tears with the loss of a loved one is a sure sign that this is *not* the correct interpretation.

Jesus' troubled groanings in the spirit and tears are comprehensible, instead, as reactions to the *lack of faith* that surrounds him. The only faith present is the one, now dashed, that Jesus could have *prevented* death if he had been there earlier. Avoidance and prevention of death are the attitudes expressed by Jesus' disciples and by Martha, now questioningly echoed by some of the Judeans (11:37). The path of discipleship, however, is not to be accompanied by any of the attitudes toward death we have seen so far. Instead, it is about *trusting that God is with us even in the face of death.* This kind of faith will lead Christians radically to resist the world's attempts to seduce them into false securities, those which try at their core to keep death at a distance. Whether the siren song of wealth, which ostensibly keeps disease, criminals, and other threats at bay, or the enticement of dominating power, which crushes threats before it can itself be crushed, the world's alternatives have in common the substitution of *violence* for faith (1:13, "born of blood;" see below). As long as Lazarus is safely in the ground, Jesus' words remain only talk, overcome by the violent threats that keep even Jesus' followers quietly obedient to the world.

When the time finally comes to put those words into action, Martha clarifies the ambiguity that remained open during her previous conversation with Jesus. The thought of the stench of death disgusts her; she cannot yet imagine the truth of Jesus' promises. After briefly scolding her lack of faith, Jesus continues to work the will of the One who sent him. He begins with a prayer, which emphasizes the reason for what he is about to do. It is an act not of self-aggrandizement but of filial loyalty intended to arouse a trusting commitment in those who witness it.

Despite the sisters' lack of faith, their brother *has* believed. He hears the voice of the son of God, the good shepherd who calls his sheep by name (10:3), and comes out. But he remains bound in the wrappings of disbelief, the cloths that were intended to diffuse the odor of decay. It is not for Jesus to undo this aspect of Lazarus's burial. Instead, he orders those within earshot to "unbind him and set him free" (11:44). Jesus can show his friends the Way; it is up to them to undo the culture of death that leaves even the living bound (cf. 21:7).

The Response of Those "Born of Blood" (John 11:45-53)

Typically, Jesus' powerful deed generates a crisis among the witnesses that leaves them divided (cf. 7:43; 9:16; 10:19). The dark possibilities incumbent upon Jesus' return to Judea will be realized now that the Pharisees have become aware of what has taken place.

The closing scene of the story—which, unfortunately, is not included in the formal lectionary reading—is an integral part of the challenge that comes to the church during this third and final scrutiny. Jesus' presence is a light shining in the darkness and, although the darkness cannot overwhelm the light (1:6), it still bears power to do evil in the world (3:19-20). Those who are "born of God" have been given the task of unbinding the violent culture of which they are a part. In the meantime, those "born of blood" continue about the task given by their own source of being.

The literal term used in the Prologue (1:13) is "born of *bloods*," an idiom referring to bloodshed and violence. The Sanhedrin, which now gathers to destroy Jesus, reveals its purpose: the preservation of the system of power and privilege that, although masked by holy ideology, is rooted in "sacred" violence. The Judean elite, when alone among themselves, admit that they are only pretending to be faithful to the covenant and its command to love God alone. Their true god is the nation-state in which they are the power bearers. Jesus' act of resurrection undermines their theology of "the last day" and threatens to subvert their hold on the people. When the divine canopy is removed, they are shown to be what they are: graspers for worldly glory. They are rulers in the reign of death, which cannot allow an unauthorized act of life-giving to go without response.

The scene John's gospel presents is laced with bitter irony. It portrays God working through those who claim to act in God's name but who know that this claim is a propagandistic lie. Their attempt to offer sacrifice in accordance with the scapegoat principle is turned upside down by the God of history. Their dream of saving the "nation" through the death of a public victim only results in their own downfall, yet does ultimately provide salvation for the "people."

This distinction between the *nation* and the *people* is at the heart of the biblical story, told again here in a new way. Its roots lie in the abandonment of God by the Israelites a millennium earlier, when they sought to "be like the nations" in having a warrior-king to rule over them (1 Sm 8). It is a struggle people of faith continue to engage in today, as the conflict between worldly security and trust in God tears at our hearts. John's gospel is unequivocal in siding with the biblical tradition that rejected power-over as idolatry unworthy of God's people. Once Israel becomes a nation, it must save itself the way nations do, through the violence of repression at home and militarism abroad (cf. 1 Kgs 4:21-26, 12:4). The gospel's claim is that in Jesus' death the nation will indeed be destroyed, but the people of God, though scattered around the earth, will be gathered into unity.

This final scrutiny challenges those within the community of Jesus' followers to put aside their last hopes in the way of the world. To become a disciple is to see past the masks of holiness and divine legitimation put on by those "born of blood." It is to break from commitment to all false births, all systems of power that seek a share of the loyalty which belongs to God alone. It is a difficult challenge, one virtually impossible for individuals acting alone. Before Easter morning the church is offered another promise, one that can provide the necessary strength to continue on the road of discipleship.

—PREACHING AND REFLECTION IDEAS—

Preaching Themes

1. Consider our attitudes toward death as presented through the attitudes of the characters in the story. Which of these attitudes are supported by the dominant culture, and which are supported by the church?

2. Consider what it would mean to live without fear of death. Share stories of particular persons of faith who have lived in

this way; for example, Joan of Arc, Dr. Martin Luther King, Jr., Archbishop Romero, or local individuals.

3. Reflect on the threats in our culture that keep people from healing the brokenness that surrounds us. If we are not faced literally with death threats, perhaps we are presented with threats of ostracism, ridicule, loss of privilege, and so on. How do we learn to overcome our fear of these threats and walk as if the Light is in us?

4. Imagine the aftermath of the Lazarus story. How might Lazarus and his sisters have felt from that day forward? What might it mean to respond to the command to "unbind him and set him free?" Consider ways in the local community that people can remove the cords of death—poverty, racism, sexism, and so on—which hold people captive.

Small Group Activities

1. As with the previous scrutiny readings, the Lazarus story can become very dramatic when acted out within a group. Invite people to choose parts to play in the drama, set either in the time of the gospel or in modern times. Allow imaginative expansion of the dialogue within the spirit of the narrative. Take time to invite reflection afterward on people's experience of the drama, either as participants or spectators.

2. Brainstorm to create a list of the ways in which the attitudes toward death portrayed in the story are manifested in our own culture. For example, consider the health care industry's attitudes toward the possibility of death. Invite discussion of how people of faith might exhibit different attitudes that model a wholeness not found in some of the other attitudes.

3. Take some quiet time to consider the experience of anticipating or experiencing the death of a loved one. Invite people to share something of their own experience of walking through that experience of death. Conclude with a ritual that invites people to offer some kind of healing touch to one another (such as laying on of hands on the head, shoulders, or hands of another along with the refrain, "Be unbound and set free").

4. Brainstorm to compile a list of the ways in which our culture reinforces a fear of the consequences of "unauthorized" healing. Invite people to share an experience of an "alternative" healing—chiropractic, acupuncture, herbal/diet therapy, prayer. What attitudes did the person bring into the experience? How did the experience change those attitudes, if it did?

Reflection Questions

1. *Personal:* What attitude do I bring to the prospect of the death of those closest to me? How would I respond to Jesus' question to Martha about believing that he is the Resurrection and the Life?

2. *Social and cultural:* What "death threats" keep me from walking into risky situations to offer a healing word or touch? Consider how the media's emphasis on violent acts, especially those which take place in neighborhoods where poverty is prevalent, keep us in fear.

3. *Ecclesial:* What attitude toward death is revealed by the local church where you live? Does the church travel to the "Judeas" of your area to take the risk of healing? Why or why not?

7

The Invitation to Become
a Footwashing Community

John 13:1-30

THE TRANSITION TO HOLY WEEK (JOHN 12:1-49)

The response to the raising of Lazarus from the dead is the crisis that propels the gospel into the narrative of Jesus' final days. In Matthew and Mark the "crime" that galvanizes the opposition to Jesus is the casting out of the money changers from the Jerusalem Temple, an outrageous act of public civil disobedience that cannot be tolerated by the defenders of the status quo. Luke provides more of a build-up of hostility throughout his gospel, declining to focus on a particular moment. But in John's gospel it is the unauthorized provision of life to the dead that constitutes the intolerable crime. And like all propagandists for an oppressive system, the Sanhedrin knows that the physical presence of Lazarus cannot be allowed to continue to undermine its version of God's story. Lazarus, too, must be destroyed (12:10).

It is in this context that we find the scene of Mary's anointing of Jesus' feet with unimaginably costly ointment (roughly the equivalent of six months' wages for a peasant). The episode is introduced with the note that it was "six days before the Passover." All that follows will occur with the moment of Passover in view. Judas Iscariot, who was but a rumor until now, takes the stage for the first time in the guise of a protester on behalf of the poor (12:4-6). The narrator and Jesus work together to refute his claim, first by undermining Judas's integrity and then by offering a counter-interpretation. Mary's act is not a waste; it is a holy ritual in preparation for Jesus' death. She reveals through her deed a clear understanding of what is about to unfold, an understanding totally lost on those at table with Jesus later the same week. She exhibits the attitude of a disciple who has learned the lesson of Lazarus: the prospect of death is not to be avoided or denied but to be prepared for.

After Jesus' Palm Sunday entrance into the Holy City, the Pharisees admit privately that their cause is lost (12:19). Of course, this recognition will not stop them from carrying out their murderous plans, any more than the Pentagon elite's inner admission that the Vietnam War was a hopeless cause prevented years of bloodshed and destruction. Once set upon the course of violence, the world's engines of power run on their own momentum. But again, John's gospel turns this into an advantage in the next scene, wherein the "Greeks" ask to see Jesus.

The advent of the Greeks means that "the hour has come for the Human One to be glorified" (12:23). No longer is the God of the covenant a private possession of Israel. Now, in the words of the Pharisees, "the world has gone after him." Through the images of the grain of wheat that bears fruit by dying and that of being "lifted up," Jesus explains before it happens the meaning of his impending passion. What appears by all worldly standards to be utter and shameful defeat will in fact be an honorable coronation, the establishment of a new kind of reign amid the reign of darkness.

The chapter continues by emphasizing the goal of inculcating discipleship among its readers and hearers. The gospel's trajectory is always a back-and-forth movement between the internal life of the church and its mission of public witness and healing. It calls people out of darkness and into the light of God, so that the world may be saved (12:47). At the heart of the thematic summary that concludes the pre-passion stage of the text is the reminder that private faith is not enough. Even some of the rulers have believed, those like Nicodemus. The sort of belief that seeks to make a compromising peace with the world is insufficient. To follow Jesus all the way through Good Friday and to Easter requires a commitment that leaves behind all forms of "the glory of humanity" (12:43). And now, the gospel will teach its audience of what the alternative consists, of what it means to love "the glory of God."

"I HAVE GIVEN YOU AN EXAMPLE" (JOHN 13:1-20)

John 13 is a turning point in the gospel. It marks the end of what some scholars call the Book of Signs (Jn 1–12) and the beginning of the Book of Glory (Jn 13–21). That is, the preceding narrative focuses on the presence of the Word in the world and the crises of response created by that presence. The three scrutinies are key moments in the encounter between God's Word and the world, three "gates" through which those who seek to become God's children must enter in order to be born again/from above.

With the Book of Glory, the time for decision has passed. The gospel's message now is for those committed to following Jesus on the last trip to Jerusalem. This journey involves risking misunderstanding, hostility, and even persecution by those defensive of an oppressive and violent status quo. It offers the promise that even when one experiences total rejection by one's community of first birth, one will be found and protected by Jesus, even if that requires reaching across the wall of death itself.

But as we know, and as the first Christians knew, Jesus himself had suffered rejection and execution at the hands of the defenders of the status quo. What real-world comfort is there for those experiencing angry repudiation to know that a "risen" Jesus is on their side? How do people of faith maintain contact with a master who has already preceded them to the other side?

The Book of Glory provides its answers to these questions in the five chapters that form what is known as the Last Supper or Farewell Discourse in John 13–17. In this, the longest continuous scene in the New Testament, Jesus prepares his community of followers for his absence. Like Moses at the end of the Exodus journey, he offers comfort and hope to people who have good reason to believe they are about to be abandoned.

Jesus begins this process of preparation with a ritual and conversation that is traditionally read on Holy Thursday, the final evening Jesus spends with the disciples before his death. No longer are the readings addressed to individual decision and commitment. Now the gospel speaks to the church as a whole in each of its local family units. Congregation by congregation, Jesus' invitation to wash one another's feet offers to believers the healing balm that can enable them to walk through the painful experiences which are to come.

Perhaps more than any other passage we have considered, the story of the footwashing is best understood only in the context of the entire gospel. Its traditionally misunderstood interpretation as a call to humble service comes from hearing its words extracted from the plot and symbolic fabric of the wider narrative. As we will see, the example Jesus gives invites believers to imitate something more profoundly hopeful than simply providing for the basic needs of our sisters and brothers. Footwashing models for the church the command to love one another as Jesus has loved us. It provides the only way in which we can walk through the pain of the passion and not find ourselves totally lost and abandoned at the foot of the cross, whether the cross of Jesus or one of our fellow disciples.

The scene begins with a lengthy introduction by the narrator, who sets out for us in 13:1-5 the contours of the microcosm present at this meal. Readers are told before Jesus speaks to his disciples that two opposing forces have prepared their representatives for final battle.

The time is both the eve of "Passover" and "the hour." The ambiguity contained in this simple temporal reference is excruciating. Passover represents the high moment of liturgical celebration for Jews throughout the world to this day, the remembering-as-present-now of the miracle of God's deliverance of a band of slaves into freedom. It is a feast rich in symbols of death and life, oppression and liberation. John's gospel has anticipated this symbolism from the moment of Jesus' arrival into the world, when John the Baptist announced him as "the Lamb of God who takes away the sin of the world" (1:29; cf. 1:36). The Passover lamb was the victim that God ordered the people captive in Egypt to kill and consume; its blood was to mark their doorposts as a sign of protection from the destroying angel who was about to come upon the oppressors (Ex 12). At the same time, the lamb image recalls the Levitical scapegoat, upon whose back the people's sins are carried into the desert (Lv 16, esp. 16:22). John's gospel has folded together these disparate images of the lamb who is eaten and whose blood is a sign of freedom with the one whose suffering removes sins from the community. Simply by noting the impending presence of Passover, these symbols for the One who is about to be crucified are brought to mind.

Of course, Passover is also a *Judean* temporal marker. The gospel accepts the symbolism and historical memory of God's powerful act of liberation associated with the feast but rejects the hypocritical use of those symbols and memory for carrying out the violence of the Judean status quo. The stance is not dissimilar from the modern one, which embraces the memory and symbols of the Prince of Peace born in poverty in a manger while rejecting the abuse of Christmas as an occasion for indulging in rampant consumerism.

In order to make clear the transformation of "Passover" from the Judean mode to the gospel mode, the time is also denoted as "the hour . . . to leave this world toward the Father." Jesus, the Lamb of God, will fulfill the feast, albeit ironically, by liberating his people from the oppression of the Judeans, who in turn do the will of their imperial overlords.

We are also told in the first verses that Jesus "loved his own in the world and loved them to the end." The twin themes of love and of being in the world will permeate the Last Supper Discourse. For the moment, they form the backdrop against which the footwashing ritual will take place. The word translated "end" also means "fulfillment" or "completion," meanings equally relevant here. That is, Jesus' final actions and teachings will give them everything disciples need to carry on in their master's absence.

In great contrast is the intentionality of Jesus' opponent, embodied as Judas Iscariot. Whereas Jesus is about to complete the work given by his own Father, God, Judas is faithful to the will of a different father, named here as the devil. One son is about completing love, the other about completing betrayal. These are the opposites the gospel presents as competing within the hearts of the disciples. It is internal betrayal, not external hatred, that is the true enemy of the faith community.

But none of this is apparent to the disciples reclining at table. What they experience in this scene begins with Jesus' rising from the table and preparing to wash their feet. The simple act of "laying down" his outer garment, which begins his action, frames the ritual, along with his "receiving" it again at the end (13:4, 12). The two verbs used in the gospel are juxtaposed only in one other place in the narrative. When Jesus, the Good Shepherd, describes the nature of his love for his sheep, he tells his hearers twice that he "lays down his life" freely and also "receives" it again freely (10:17-18). In the footwashing episode the "outer garment" would, to a Hellenistic audience—now included in the community with the coming of the "hour" (12:20-23)—be a fitting metaphor for Jesus' body, his external life. We should therefore hear this scene in the death/resurrection context that frames all of Holy Week. In a sense, the act of footwashing takes place *between* death and resurrection, during a liminal phase in the life both of Jesus and of his community.

Finally, the ritual itself is narrated, as Jesus proceeds around the room washing and drying his disciples' feet. When it becomes Simon Peter's turn, there is resistance. Before Peter can express his disgust at the prospect of having his master wash his feet, Jesus tells him, "You do not know now what I am doing, but you will know after these things." We are thus prepared to interpret Peter's own understanding of the act as the wrong interpretation. This recognition is key to following the logic of the scene. But what is it about the prospect of having his feet washed that so repels Peter that he lashes out in adamant refusal to cooperate?

It was common practice for a host in the ancient world to provide a bowl in which a guest could get his feet washed. If the host had a servant, it would be the servant's role to wash the guest's feet; otherwise, the guest could wash his own feet. It would certainly *not* be expected that the host would do the washing. Hospitality would not require humiliation of the host. Honor between host and guest would be maintained by the sheer provision of the bowl and towel.

More generally in teacher/disciple relationships, the disciples would always be in a subservient social role to their teacher. The student role is not itself one requiring humiliation, but it would require service to the master as repayment for the teaching services provided to the disciple. Again, it would never be considered that a master would perform dishonoring acts of service for his students.

This cultural code would form at least some of the mind-set of Peter as he watched with horror as his master approached. The other disciples might have been too overwhelmed by the shock of what was happening to object, but Simon Peter was not about to allow the continuation of this humiliating scene. Even if it meant embarrassing Jesus by speaking harshly to him in front of the community, the loss of honor to the master would be less in such a rebuke than in Peter's acceptance of the act of footwashing.

That is, Simon Peter understood Jesus' act as one of humble service that reversed the cultural hierarchy between master and disciple. Yet Jesus says clearly that *Peter's interpretation is wrong!* Countless Holy Thursday homilies have shown that the church generally has followed Peter in misunderstanding the meaning of footwashing. A lesson in humble service would be completely out of place in this location in the gospel narrative and ill-fitting with the death/resurrection context so carefully crafted by the narrator. To perceive the deeper meaning of the passage, we must continue and listen to Jesus' own explanation.

Jesus' first response to Peter's resistance is to be equally adamant. If Peter imagines he is protecting a master gone mad, Jesus insists that Peter's participation is essential to his remaining a part of Jesus' "inheritance." The term echoes the Exodus theme of requiring obedience to God's commandments as a prerequisite for membership in the tribal inheritance of Israel (the Hebrew word for "inheritance" is used over two hundred times in the Hebrew scriptures). When Peter realizes he is on the edge of excommunication, he relents in typically Petrine hyperbolic style.

Jesus responds next by distinguishing *washing* from *bathing*. The footwashing is not a ritual akin to the Judean bathing, which expiated legal impurity. Rather, it is an act that, like baptism, uses water to bind together a community. In this context Jesus makes the first suggestion that the act serves as an antidote to the betrayal he and they are about to experience.

He next responds to the implicit (mis)understanding of Peter and the other disciples. He who is "Lord and teacher" has washed their feet, in shocking violation of their expectations. But the central purpose of the act is not from Lord/teacher to disciple but from disciple to disciple. The example is for the community. The word translated "example" is rare in the New Testament, but was used in the Septuagint in the context of providing an example to youth of *how to die*. For example, we find a good instance in 2 Maccabees 6:28, 31, where Eleazer describes his own impending demise:

> "Therefore, by manfully giving up my life now, I will prove myself worthy of my old age, and I will leave to the young a noble *example* of how to die willingly and generously for the revered and holy laws." . . . This is how he died, leaving in his death a model of courage and an unforgettable *example* of virtue not only for the young but for the whole nation (emphasis added).

The disciples are unlikely, though, to have picked up this clue from Jesus' words. John's gospel repeats many times that the community did not understand the relationship between Jesus' actions and words and Hebrew scripture until after the resurrection. For now, this is a clue only for alert readers of the text, not for characters in the story.

A second time Jesus suggests the presence of a betrayer in the midst of the group, providing his own link with Hebrew scripture (13:18). Finally, with deep emotion parallel to that which he experienced at the lack of faith in Bethany (11:33), Jesus "witnessed" to the betrayer's presence. And now, for the first time, someone other than Peter reacts. As a group the disciples "were looking into one another, at a loss about whom he was speaking." How can this be? Can we imagine traveling with a small group of people from town to town over a long period of time and being so ignorant of one another as to be without a clue as to the presence of a betrayer in our midst?

At this crucial juncture the narrator introduces a character who will be key to all that follows, "the one whom Jesus loved," usually referred to as the Beloved Disciple. He is described as reclining in a position of deepest intimacy with his master, a position parallel to that of Jesus to the Father (1:18). Even this one has no idea who the betrayer is! It requires an act of symbolic identification by Jesus to connect the accusation to Judas. Incredibly, even after this identification the narrator tells us that "no one at the table knew" why Jesus told Judas to complete his deed quickly, with some so out of touch as to imagine that Jesus was calling for a last-minute shopping errand or gift to charity. It is with this terrible revelation of ignorance that the betrayer exits, and the "night" begins.

What are we to make of this sequence in relation to the meaning of footwashing? With the entire scene in mind, we must step back to consider the theme that dominates the overall context. The passage begins with a statement of Jesus' complete *knowledge* and ends with one of the disciples' utter *ignorance*. Jesus "knows" it is his hour, that the Father has given all things into his hands, that he has come forth from God and is going to God, and what he himself is to do at this moment. The disciples, in diametrical contrast, do not know the purpose of the footwashing, the identity of the betrayer, the nature of their own moral character, or Jesus' own direction in his mission. As the Last Supper Discourse continues to unfold, their ignorance will expand to include Peter's lack of self-awareness (13:37-38), their ignorance of "the way" (14:5), Philip's lack of understanding of the identity between Jesus and the Father (14:8), and what it is that has happened which will change everything (14:22).

This opposition between Jesus' perfect awareness and the disciples' near perfect lack of awareness is not, however, a matter of deficiency in doctrine or other intellectual deficits. Rather, the footwashing scene painfully reveals that what they are missing is not head knowledge but heart knowledge. It is *biblical* knowledge that is absent. Just as the first man "knew" the first woman in the biblical metaphor for sexual intercourse (Gn 4:1), the disciples' problem is not a failure of theology but a failure of *intimacy*. And this is where footwashing provides the antidote that will prepare them for Jesus' absence. The example that Jesus has given them is *of how to prepare one another for the journey through rejection and even death by developing community intimacy that overcomes individual fear with mutual love.*

The disciples in the story, like many in the church throughout history, are so focused on Jesus that they have forgotten to pay attention to each other. This is the only explanation for their shocking inability to identify the betrayer. We too, in our North American individualistic culture, rarely open ourselves to our fellow believers enough to know what is in each other's heart. We are not usually encouraged to do so, and even if we were, who would dare to trust enough?

The footwashing ritual invites disciples, then and now, to break through our cultural and psychological barriers to intimacy and learn tenderly to accept one another as we are. Footwashing calls us to reveal a part of ourselves that is usually hidden. Even when our feet are exposed, they are not the focal point of attention. How often do we make eye-foot—let alone hand-foot—contact with one another? As a nurse friend has told me, even in the hospital people will often remove their clothes but leave their socks on, and not just because the floor is cold! Feet are an apt symbol for the reality of ourselves. We can do little to change the appearance of our feet. If our toes are crooked, our skin callused, our toenails discolored, that is the way people will see our feet no matter what we do. To invite people to look at, to wash, to care for our feet is to invite them to accept us as we are.

There is also a powerful biblical metaphor underlying Jesus' choice of footwashing as a symbolic invitation to intimacy. We may recall that when Moses first encountered God at the burning bush, God ordered Moses to "remove the sandals from your feet, for the place on which you are standing is holy ground" (Ex 3:5). Subsequently, Moses commanded the placing of a water bowl between the altar and the sanctuary for Aaron and his sons to wash their feet (Ex 30:19). Building on that connection, the Jerusalem priests who entered the Holy of Holies in the Temple were met with a water basin with which to wash their feet in preparation for their encounter with God. Thus, footwashing was traditionally understood as an act performed by those about to meet God. For the Judeans, this invitation was limited to the Jerusalem priestly elite. For John's gospel, the invitation is extended to the entire faith community without distinction. For the Judeans, God was found in the ritual "re-membering" of the community through the sacrificial system of the Jerusalem Temple. For the Johannine Christians, God was to be found in the "re-membering" of the community through the ritual of footwashing, which was to occur during the community's celebration of the breaking of the bread.

Putting our symbols together, we find that the gospel anticipates the fulfillment of this invitation in two contexts. In the act of intimacy involved in community life, disciples wash one another's feet to find God within the community. Eventually, this will be narrated by their experience of the risen Jesus "in their midst" (20:19). Second, footwashing is an "example" with which they can prepare one another to die a noble death, and hence, like Lazarus, find God with them on the other side of the grave.

Footwashing provides the strength necessary to commit to living out the challenges presented by the Prologue "nots" (1:13), as narrated in the dramas of John 4, 9, and 11. If one is to reject the world's forms of "birth" in favor of being born again/from above of God, one needs the support and trust that comes from life within a community of disciples living in intimacy with one another. When Jesus continues to speak at the end of chapter 13, he immediately proceeds to this theme, giving them "a new commandment: love one another as I have loved you" (13:34). When he repeats this commandment later in the Last Supper Discourse, he will elaborate on it to add that "no one has greater love than this: to lay down one's life for one's friends. You are my friends if you do what I am commanding you" (15:13-14). Just as Jesus, the Good Shepherd, shows his love for the sheep in this way, so are the disciples to follow this example. The only way one can gain the courage to be willing to take this loving risk is by living in the kind of intimacy that footwashing anticipates.

We can see that in every sense of the term John's gospel intends footwashing to be what the church would later call a sacrament. It is a ritual act through which God provides grace needed by individuals and by the community as a whole to live out the gospel in a hostile world. Through the ordinary materials of water, basin, and towel, Jesus calls his followers to remind one another of a central aspect of what it means to be church. To be able to go out into a hostile world in witness to God's love requires the awareness that one is supported in both the sending and the returning. It is a kind of breathing out and breathing in that forms equal parts of the rhythm of discipleship. Without footwashing (as well as eucharist) the mission becomes one of grim determination, without joy or hope. Without the mission, the call to intimacy can easily be reduced to "personal growth" or "group support" that serves nothing beyond one's narcissistic desires. Only in the harmonious balance presented by the Last Supper Discourse can the grace offered by the footwashing ritual be put to the use the gospel anticipates: the continuation of the mission of the Word in the world. To exhort the church to carry out this task is the purpose of the remainder of the Last Supper Discourse.

—Preaching and Reflection Ideas—

Preaching themes

1. Reflect on the placement of the footwashing episode in the journey of Lent. On the eve of betrayal and death Jesus prepares his community to go on without him. Consider the Christian community's call to help one another prepare for the loss of loved ones, whether through natural causes or political repression. Provide examples of how this might work in parts of the world where death threats are an everyday reality.

2. Consider the challenge of coming to "know one another." Point out examples of how our lives are structured to prevent the development of intimacy; for example, workplace settings that make personal sharing among workers inappropriate; private housing and transportation that "protect" us from contact with others in our neighborhood; geographic dispersal of families; linear rows of church pews that lead us to "know" the backs of the heads of those in front of us.

3. Reflect on the acceptance of the risk of betrayal within the Christian community. How does the fear that we might get hurt prevent us from taking the risk of exposing ourselves to one another? Consider footwashing as an invitation to be washed clean of that fear.

4. Consider the image of death as meeting God. The disciples' fear of losing Jesus—and of their own deaths—implicitly rejected the idea that dying brought one even closer to God. How do we live out the call to trust that death is not an ultimate ending but simply a transition from one kind of relationship with God to another?

Small Group Activities

Note: It is highly recommended that a group not wash one another's feet unless the members are committed to continuing in relationship with one another. Practicing footwashing in a setting where no real intimacy is expected among participants risks falsifying and trivializing the ritual.

1. Take some quiet time individually to consider our attitudes toward and experiences of intimacy. Has this led to betrayal? Has it led to deeper trust? Invite sharing among those who are willing. Be particularly sensitive to respecting people's feelings and experiences on this most personal of topics.

2. Discuss how our culture prepares for death; for example, gathering around a hospital or other death bed; planning liturgies or other ritual gatherings after death; rites of anointing. Consider whether we prepare only those in imminent danger of passing or also those in good health but faced with possibly risky situations, such as travel to a dangerous location.

3. Brainstorm ways in which the footwashing ritual could become a regular part of the life of the church. Should it be reserved for Holy Thursday and for a select group of the congregation? How might it be used in less formal settings than weekly liturgy, such as initiation of councils or other church groups, or within families?

Reflection Questions

1. *Personal:* What are my own feelings about intimacy? Do I seek it out or resist it when it is offered? Reflect on one intimate relationship in which I participate. Consider the experience of being betrayed, and what my response to that experience may have been in being invited into subsequent intimate relationships.

2. *Social and cultural:* How does one's local cultural situation support or prevent intimacy? What images from mass media and culture come to mind in considering the dominant culture's attitudes toward really knowing other people?

3. *Ecclesial:* How has footwashing been experienced in your congregation? Who washed and who was washed? What meaning was attached to the ritual? How might it be different if understood as communal preparation for facing the possibility of death?

8

The Last Supper Discourse

Mystagogia for the Church

The church's lectionary breaks John 13–17 into two parts. The footwashing story is proclaimed at the end of Lent, while the remainder of the Last Supper Discourse is saved for the period between Easter and Pentecost. In so doing, the church recognizes that Jesus' commands and exhortations, ostensibly proclaimed on the eve of his death, were only remembered and understood in light of the Easter experience with the assistance of the Paraclete (14:26, 15:26).

The passages are difficult reading for the uninitiated. The rhythm of repeated words and tightly structured speeches can seem boring to our untrained ears. Conditioned as we are by television to fast action and quick scene changes, the slow, deliberate pace of the Last Supper Discourse can feel like the pattern of a European art film. But once we take the time to meditate on Jesus' words and the disciples' confused questions, the images of the discourse break through the fog and reveal an edifice in which the church can find its home.

The discourse begins with Jesus' address to the disciples with the fittingly intimate term, "little children" (13:33). This brings forward both the call to community intimacy implicit in the ritual footwashing and the Prologue invitation to become children of God (1:12). The central interlocking themes of the entire discourse are then presented immediately: 1) Jesus is going away and, for now, "where I am going you cannot come" (13:34); 2) the disciples are to "love one another, as I have loved you" (13:34); and 3) "by this all will know that you are my disciples" (13:35). These statements are not mere juxtapositions. Rather, Jesus is trying to teach them (and us) that the only way for Christians to cope with Jesus' absence is to find his presence in the practice of mutual love within the church itself. This is the "breathing in" of Christian life. At the same time, this love is to be visible in the world, as a witness to the possibility of a way of life different from the "darkness" of the world. This taking of the community's experience of the power of love into the world is the "breathing out" that completes the rhythm of gospel life.

The disciples' response to this command and promise is fear and confusion, expressed through a series of ironic and darkly humorous questions. Peter begins with a pair of queries that reveal his total ignorance of both Jesus' destiny and his own lack of fidelity. But lest Peter feel alone in his confusion, Thomas follows with his confession, apparently on behalf of all, that "we do not know where you are going; how can we know the way?" (14:5). On the heels of this comes Philip, who, again speaking in the plural, calls for a revelation of the Father as "sufficient" proof that they should believe Jesus' words (14:8). Finally, Judas, "not Iscariot," wonders aloud about the event that has taken place, which supposedly is to justify a change in Jesus' revelatory script (14:22).

The interspersing of these questions helps readers, who may be harboring similar questions, not to feel so removed from the scene. The discourse does not portray a community that clearly understands and takes up Jesus' commands. Jesus' words will be understood only in the course of trying to live them out. They will remain mysterious and impenetrable so long as they are considered only by thinking about them while sitting around a table. When the community has breathed together (*con-spired*) a few times in the love/witness cycle, it will begin to see the bright light that Jesus' words offer.

In order to strengthen the community to take the risk of Christian practice, Jesus gives the disciples a gift that John's gospel calls the Paraclete. The Greek root contains the double meaning of "comforter" and "advocate." Both functions are attributed to this new presence, which is also called "the spirit of truth" and "the holy spirit" (14:17, 26). That is, the Paraclete is there for the church in both the breathing in (comfort) and breathing out (advocacy). Each of these functions should be considered separately.

As *comforter*, the Paraclete's primary power is to remind the community members of what Jesus has told them and to teach them even more of what they need to know but are as yet unable to bear (14:26, 16:12-13). In effect, the Paraclete leads the church in reflecting on scripture and its relationship to the church's own experience. The gospel provides no official structure for church life. For John, *apostle* is a verb (Greek, *apostellō*, "to send forth"), not a noun. In place of reliance on the reproduction of the sort of elite leadership that the gospel sees as a key to the errors of Judean ideology, the gospel builds the church around the leadership of the Paraclete/Spirit, which "blows where it wills" (3:8). The Paraclete comforts the church by helping it to interpret its difficult experience in light of Jesus' own life and words. Over and over again the Paraclete reminds the church of its call to be united with God as Jesus was.

The flip side of the Paraclete's function is that of *advocacy*. A key theme that emerges in the second part of the Last Supper Discourse is that faithfulness to Jesus will result in "hate" and persecution by "the world," represented in court by Satan, the accuser, "the ruler of this world" (hate/persecution: 15:18-25, 16:1-4; ruler of this world: 14:30, 16:11). Jesus expressly names the Paraclete as the one who will help guide the church through this painful experience (15:26, 16:8-11). This guidance will take the form of "witness" to and "convicting" of the world. Without the Paraclete, the disciples are merely frightened children in the face of parental criticism. But with the advocacy of the Spirit, the church is called to a maturity that fearlessly speaks truth to power regardless of the consequences. This speech will name the world's sin and call the world to repentance. It is important to recall that John's gospel does not settle for a holier-than-thou, us-against-the-world sort of sectarianism. Rather, it aims to bring the world into the light of God's presence and to heal it of its sinfulness (3:16, 16:8-11).

This mission of the church to be "*in* the world" but not "*of* the world" is another essential lesson taught in the Last Supper

Discourse. The discourse ends with Jesus' prayer to his Father on behalf of his disciples. Throughout this prayer Jesus emphasizes to the disciples that they are to replace him as God's presence in the world (17:11, 13, 15-18, 23). The most difficult challenge of John's gospel is to walk this balancing act of discipleship. It would be much easier to take one of the two escape routes from this narrow path, both of which the gospel clearly rejects. The first is the *Nicodemus option*: to be in the world *and* of the world, while claiming secretly to be a disciple. The second is the *Qumran option*: to be neither in the world *nor* of the world. The urge to build the city of God far from the city of humanity is a powerful temptation for those who have tasted the blood spilled by the world's violence. But Jesus expressly asks God "not to take them out of the world, but to protect them from the evil one" (17:15). The church's mission is irrevocably among the broken bones and cracked pavement of the world's streets. While the rhythm of witnessing and healing requires the availability of "safe houses" apart from the pain and threats (e.g., 10:39-40), the discipleship community is called to return to its home away from home in the midst of the world.

The final theme of the Last Supper Discourse is the invitation to the community to call on the power of *prayer*. Jesus assures the disciples that if they are "in" his "name," their prayers will be heard and answered (14:13-14, 16:23-24). Jesus' name is not a magic talisman by which believers can obtain material wealth or other signs of worldly success. Rather, being in Jesus' name is a way of saying that one's life is conformed to Jesus' life, obedient to the One Jesus called Father. For such a person, prayer is a form of communication between lovers. How can the Lover not respond to the needs and desires of the beloved?

The images of unity between God and disciple that weave the thread that holds the Last Supper Discourse together are what lead many interpreters of John's gospel to read it as a mystical narrative. There is no doubt that the gospel beckons readers to an intimate relationship with God that does not require the mediation of Pharisees or priests. The God whom Jesus calls Father is immediately available to those who trust in Jesus' name. But it is important to remember that the gospel's images of divine/human unity are not presented for the sake of invoking individual ecstasy. Jesus' pronouns are almost always plural, spoken to encourage the *church's* intimacy with God. And this communal intimacy is always for the sake of providing witness to the world, the "breathing out" aspect of Christian life. The poetic verses that come near the close of the discourse illustrate this linkage beautifully:

> Not about these only am I praying, but also about
> the ones trusting in me through their word:
> so that all may be one, just as you, Father are in
> me, and I in you;
> so that they also may be in us,
> so that the world might believe that you sent me.
> (John 17:20-21)

For the early Christian communities, the Last Supper Discourse exhorted them to be in the same relationship with God as was Jesus during his earthly sojourn. Many Christians found themselves facing the identical fate as their Master, whether by crucifixion or some other form of state execution. The discourse became a constant source of hope and comfort amid a church life that encountered constant threats of rejection and persecution. If these passages seem distant and boring to many in the North American church today, perhaps it is because our Christian life does not confront us with these threats. Rather than witnessing to the world of the possibility of love and intimacy, the church has all too often made a compromised peace with the world. Like Nicodemus, it has claimed Jesus as a teacher from God, while accepting the glory the world offers. Each year between Easter and Pentecost these passages call us to a new commitment to the Christian conspiracy. They remind us that our vocation is "in" but not "of" the world, precisely because God's love for the world cannot be fulfilled in an atmosphere of violence, blindness, and fear. Just as the great mystics of old, whose experience of God's presence led them to challenge injustice of both church and state, we in the church today are invited by these stories to become prophetic mystics, bound together by an intimacy that trusts that the Paraclete is with us through it all.

—Preaching and Reflection Ideas—

Fifth Sunday of Easter (John 13:31-35)

Preaching Themes

1. Consider the command to love one another in the broader context of the Last Supper Discourse (Jn 15:12-13). Share stories of people laying down their lives for one another, whether literally or metaphorically. Imagine what the church's witness would do for the world if Christians really lived in accordance with Jesus' commandment.

2. Reflect on the idea of the glory of God. What images or feelings do we have about the notion of glory? Consider Jesus' obedience to God's commandment that led to his death as somehow revealing glory. Reflect on how faith leads us to interpret life with a different lens from the world's, in finding glory in events which the world sees as humiliating.

Small Group Activities

1. Take some quiet time to reflect on an experience of finding that the "world" has recognized a community of which you are (or were) a part by its love for one another. Was the community a church, a family, or some other kind of group? Invite people to share their individual experiences. Close with a ritual that includes a symbol of the current group's attempt to love one another, if appropriate to the developmental stage and commitment of the group.

2. Discuss the ideas and/or feelings people in the group have about the concept of glory. What does it mean to glorify God? Is such a concept meaningful in our culture? What if we substituted the term *honor* for *glory*, which in biblical Greek are closely related words?

Reflection Questions

1. *Personal:* How have I been a sign to the world of the presence of God's love through my love of others? What factors in my

personal attitudes and experiences make it easy or difficult to develop loving relationships with others?

2. *Social and cultural:* How would a community that lives in mutual love be perceived by our culture? Consider media caricatures of cults and other alternative-lifestyle communities.

3. *Ecclesial:* Is your church perceived in your cultural location as a community grounded in mutual love? If not, how do you think those not a part of the church perceive it? How might that be different from how the church members perceive themselves? If there is a divergence between "inside" and "outside" perspectives, what are the factors that make for those different points of view?

Sixth Sunday of Easter (John 14:23-29)

Preaching Themes

1. Consider the concept of peace. Give examples of the world's ideas about peace, for example, the absence of war maintained through mutual threat, repression of conflict or other disharmony, control by the powerful of those who would "make waves." Imagine what Jesus' peace would look like in our world, flowing from the biblical concept of *shalom* as wholeness of person and society.

2. Reflect on the role of the Holy Spirit as comforter and as advocate. How does trust in the Spirit's presence serve to heal the church of its fear of the world? How does such trust empower disciples to speak boldly in public without fear of incompetence or reprisal?

Small Group Activities

1. Brainstorm to create a list of possible meanings of the word *peace*. If a concordance is available, find some biblical passages in which the word is used and read them, considering the meaning of peace suggested by each reading. Discuss which of these meanings come under the heading "the world's peace" and which come under the heading "Jesus' peace." What fac-

tors led you to place each meaning in one or the other category?

2. Take some quiet time to consider an experience in which individuals sensed the presence of what you call "the Holy Spirit." Was it an experience of comfort, of advocacy, or of something else? Invite people to share something of their experience. Close with a ritual that involves fire or wind moving within the group, such as a candle passed around, a circulating fan, or something similar.

Reflection Questions

1. *Personal:* Recall a situation in which you felt at peace. What was going on in your life at the time? Was your experience "the world's peace" (relief that a conflict was avoided through denial) or Jesus' peace (a deep sense of God's presence within)?

2. *Social and cultural:* Consider statements from politicians or other government officials about the presence of peace. What makes for peace in the speaker's frame of reference? How would the culture be concretely different if Jesus' idea of peace were widely practiced?

3. *Ecclesial:* What does it mean to say that the Holy Spirit is always with the church? How can we discern the Spirit's presence in a given situation (cf. 1 Jn 4:1)?

9

The Passion of Jesus
according to John

Each gospel presents a unique account of Jesus' arrest, trial, execution and burial, together known as passion narratives. More than perhaps any other aspects of the gospels, the passion narratives combine historical and cultural detail with creative writing. The portraits of Jesus and his opponents that emerge from each gospel vary tremendously.

Many scholars concerned with historical accuracy have denigrated John's gospel's passion narrative because of its supposed unlikely presentation of the relationship between Jerusalem and Rome in sharing responsibility for Jesus' death. There is no doubt that John's gospel presents its version in a highly stylized, dramatic fashion. Scenes such as the conversation between Jesus and Pilate include details that seem unavailable to Christian witnesses without relying on all-purpose attribution such as the Holy Spirit. Whatever one may conclude about the historicity of the story, the church has long chosen it as the version to be proclaimed on Good Friday. In so doing, it announces its trust in the story as of utmost importance to the Christian community's understanding of Jesus and of itself. The narrative's rich supply of irony and political drama reward the closest attention one can give to its details of narration, characterization, plot, and scenic design.

The highly organized structure of the fourth gospel's passion narrative reminds us throughout that the entire story has been orchestrated by the Word of God, not by the machination of the

Judeans and the Roman governor. Those who appear in charge, as Jesus tells Pilate, "would have no authority . . . if it had not been given from above" (19:11). Just as God used the Babylonians to punish the wayward Israelites and used the Persian king Cyrus to be their messiah (Is 45:1), so God now uses the worldly powers to teach the covenant people once again what it means to be children of God and what it means to give up that claim in exchange for another paternity.

"STANDING WITH THEM": JESUS BETRAYED (JOHN 18:1-12)

Jesus is in charge of the drama from the first words of the passion, which the narrative begins by stating that "Jesus came out with his disciples." He crosses the Kidron Valley, a place mentioned only here in the New Testament but with a foreboding echo from Hebrew scripture: "On the day you go out across the Kidron Valley, know for certain you shall die" (1 Kgs 2:37).

They enter a garden that has been a common meeting place for the community. Immediately Judas—characterized always as "the betrayer"—is brought upon the scene as one who knew the place from participation in previous intimate gatherings of the discipleship group. The scene is set up as a messianic battle. The son of God comes with his people, and the "son of perdition" (17:12) with his own troops. Judas's band includes Roman soldiers—the term used refers to the entire military cohort available to the Roman governor, between two hundred and six hundred men—and Judean police, indicating that the conspiracy between empire and colony has already been established. This contrasts with the synoptic accounts, which suggest that Rome was only reluctantly dragged into the condemnation of Jesus, and only because of the need to make an on-the-spot decision when confronted with the charge against Jesus. John's gospel makes clear that Rome and Jerusalem are acting together from the first moment, but even this conspiracy is being orchestrated by Judas, the tool of the devil (13:2, 27). It is a battle of "sons," each loyal to his father's will.

The scene takes a turn for the ironic with the notation that the arresting party comes with "torches and lamps" along with their weapons. They bring weak human lights as they stumble in the dark toward the one who is the Light of the world!

Once again, the narrator underscores Jesus' clear understanding of the situation as he steps forward to initiate the conversation (18:4). In typical Johannine fashion, Jesus' question is both ordinary and profound: "Whom are you seeking?" It recalls the initial messianic discipleship question asked in 1:38. With his freedom on the line, Jesus asks a crisis-generating question, one that challenges his opponents to reveal their theological hope. They are "from below," however, and interpret his query on the "earthly" level, identifying only "Jesus the Nazarene" as the object of their quest.

Again, the dual-level drama invites a profound response, as Jesus says, "I AM [*egō eimi*]." Before they can react, the narrator interjects the fact that "Judas the betrayer was standing with them." We recall that the term "with them" is a Johannine signal for one's deepest loyalty (9:40). In the presence of I AM, Judas remains aligned with the worldly powers. His betrayal is absolute and irrevocable. With the narrative placement of Judas between Jesus' two "I AM" statements, those with eyes to see discover that despite Judas's imperial and Judean support, he is "surrounded" by God's presence. At the earthly level, Jesus is trapped by the powers of the world. At the heavenly level it is the betrayer who is trapped, unable to escape from the Holy One.

One might expect Jesus' self-identification to lead to his immediate arrest. Surprisingly, though, the band of soldiers and police does perceive, however dimly, the power of Jesus' I AM, and, after retreating (literally, "they went off to the things behind," cf. 6:66) falls to the ground as a single entity. The scene is both a dramatic epiphany of the Human One and a political cartoon. The pure Word of God can bowl over both Rome and Jerusalem in a single stroke!

Jesus, totally in charge of the action, repeats his question and gets the identical answer. Their moment of revelatory *tremendum* is overcome by their political allegiance. John's gospel recognizes that true conversion does not happen instantly because of the experience of signs and wonders (2:23-24; 4:48). Rather, it is the ongoing process modeled by the once blind one that gradually leads a person from initial epiphany to full commitment. The soldiers and police are unable to break out of their long-standing roles just because of their momentary encounter with I AM.

The focus of the narrative is not on their reaction, though, but on Jesus' fulfillment of scripture, both Hebrew tradition and the scripture unfolding before readers' eyes. Before he goes to confront the powers, the Good Shepherd protects his sheep from the thieves and plunderers (10:8-15, 17:12).

Then, just as the scene seems completely within Jesus' serene control, Simon Peter bursts forth with a sword. His ignorance is once more revealed: rather than laying down his own life as he predicted he would, he attempts to take the life of another, an attempt that will backfire with tragicomic irony at the priestly fireside. Jesus quickly puts a stop to the revolutionary violence, claiming "the cup that the Father has given me" as the proper script to be fulfilled. The juxtaposition of Jesus' prayerful clarity of purpose with Peter's confusion underscores the distance the church has to go to attain the life to which it is called in the Last Supper Discourse.

With Peter's act of violence, the revelatory spell over the arresting party is broken. They are quickly reminded of their purpose, and of why they brought their own weapons on this night-time foray to the garden. Again acting as a unit, the soldiers and police seize their prey. The fate of the disciples is left hanging dramatically in the air.

"WHY QUESTION ME? QUESTION THOSE WHO HEARD ME" (JOHN 18:13-27)

The passage narrating the confrontation between Jesus and the Judean authorities focuses on the contrast between Jesus' witness and Peter's denial. Peter's opportunity to respond to the "charge" against him comes first, and when Jesus does speak, he refers the authorities to the testimony of those to whom he has spoken publicly. Again we see how the gospel's emphasis is on the importance of discipleship over christology. It is all too easy on Good Friday to distance ourselves from Jesus' pain. Most of us in our culture do not experience nighttime interrogations, nor is the threat of state execution in the air. With the latest Amnesty International report of torture in distant lands, we can easily feel sorry for "them." And we can empathize with Jesus' suffering and imagine the horror of the crucifixion nails in our hands. But John's gospel pulls us closer into the scene than we might like. Jesus expected and was prepared for his hour before the authorities. Peter, though, like us, thought he could watch from a distance, remaining warm by the fireside while Jesus is in the dock. The story reminds us that Good Friday is the hour for *our* witness as well as for Jesus', and we had better be prepared if we wish to avoid identifying too closely with the lead disciple.

The narrator introduces the double scene with a curious description of the priestly leadership. Annas, the chief priest emeritus, who had been replaced over the years by a succession of Rome-appointed lackeys, is revealed to remain in power despite the imperial attempt at control. The gospel recognizes that the Judean elite have their own determinants of power independent of Roman manipulation. Annas is the power behind the official authority of his son-in-law, Caiaphas. We are immediately reminded of the latter's "prophetic" role in ironically providing the reason for Jesus' impending death (11:50-51, 18:13-14).

Before this dramatic confrontation can take place, the narrator transfers us from the priestly house to outside the courtyard, where Simon Peter and "another disciple" were following Jesus. Commentators have long wondered about the identity of Peter's mysterious companion, refusing to allow the gospel to leave him anonymous. While the gospel withholds his name, it gives us another piece of important information: he is "known to the chief priest," a fact repeated for emphasis in the next verse. Whoever the other disciple is, he walks among the elite, which gives him access to the courtyard. Whether this disciple is known to the chief priest *as a disciple*, however, is left ambiguous. It seems unlikely, given the official hostility against Jesus and the previous mockery of the idea that one of "the rulers" might believe in him (7:48), that a known disciple among the elite would be allowed so close to the interrogation room. One possibility is that this other disciple is someone like Nicodemus, who might well be known to both the chief priest and to Simon Peter. There appears to be no other satisfactory explanation for how one of Jesus' community might be able to come so near to the inner sanctum of Judean power.

Before Peter can follow this elite disciple into the courtyard, though, he is confronted by a person at the opposite end of the social spectrum: the servant girl who serves as doorkeeper. It is ironic that while Jesus testifies before the chief priest, his disciple is put on trial by a servant girl. It is also a suggestion that the trial Jesus will undergo is in an illegal "kangaroo court," for only *men* were authorized to be doorkeepers at the Temple where such trials were supposed to be held *during the day*. Those who will claim before Pilate to be concerned only with the enforcement of Torah are revealed beforehand to be political hypocrites, willing to use any means necessary to accomplish their ends.

But for now, the attention is on Peter. The question the portress puts to him is straightforward, although the tone with which she says it is not. It may be the voice of a harried bureaucrat: "Not another one I have to deal with!" Or it could be the curiosity of someone who has heard rumors about this band of dissidents and is interested in meeting one for herself. In whatever way Peter hears it, his answer is sharp: "I am not!" The Greek phrase— *ouk eimi*—expresses the precise opposite of Jesus' own self-identification—*egō eimi*—before the arresting party. His words express a paradoxically true statement. The fact that he denies Jesus indicates that he is in fact *not* a disciple, even if he thinks that his statement is a lie. The one who promised to lay down his life for his Master has failed the first test of his discipleship.

After the first denial, we are given more description of the scene: a fireside at which the servants and police are warming themselves against the chilly, nighttime air. And, like a sword thrust, the narrator strikes at Peter by noting that he "stood with them, warming himself." Just as Judas "stood with" the Roman soldiers and Judean police at Jesus' arrest, so now Peter stands with the police during Jesus' trial. Both his words and his actions reveal his lack of solidarity with his captive Lord.

Having set up this terrible scene outside the courtyard, the narrator returns us to the inside, where Jesus is being questioned by the chief priest "about his disciples and about his teaching." It is important to notice that Jesus is not challenged directly about his messianic claims, which were the supposed basis for the initial anger against him (5:18). The authorities have already decided to kill Jesus; what remains to be found out prior to the execution is the nature of the discipleship community. Perhaps if Jesus "names names" they will let him go.

Jesus, of course, has no interest in cooperating with their political machinations. He will not testify on behalf of the faith of others. Instead, he tells his interrogator, "I have spoken openly to the world; I always taught in synagogue and in the Temple, where all the Judeans are coming together, and I spoke nothing in secret. Why are you questioning me? Question the ones having heard what I spoke to them. See! These know what I said" (18:20-21). Once again, the emphasis is drawn away from Jesus and toward his disciples, including those of us listening to the Good Friday story. Jesus has given his witness boldly in the synagogue at Capernaum, in the Temple on Tabernacles and Chanukah, and on numerous sabbaths. He will not waste his words before an insincere audience. Instead, he points toward what he spent the Last Supper Discourse preparing his disciples for: the "hour" when they/we will be called on to witness to the world.

The police officer standing by responds with a blatant challenge to Jesus' honor by slapping him in the face. He has perceived Jesus' words as an insult to the chief priest, who does not lower himself to respond directly to Jesus' challenge. But what is it about Jesus' statement that has so upset the police?

If we look carefully at the juxtaposition of Jesus' words, we can see precisely where the insult lies. Jesus' statement forms two parallel lines, a familiar construction from Hebrew poetry and rhetoric common to the psalms and the prophets. In so doing, he has equated "the world" with the "synagogue and Temple." Of course, one of the Judeans' primary self-identifying features is that they are different from others, a people set apart from "the world" through the practice of Torah. Jesus' statement insultingly—albeit accurately—points out their *lack* of distinction from the world. The police officer's slap attempts to protect the honor of the chief priest from the brunt of this insult.

Jesus immediately challenges the justice of the action, claiming the truth of his testimony. It is an audaciously bold piece of public witness, unheard of before the power of the Sanhedrin, which expected and normally received cringing obedience from those brought before it accused of crimes. How many of us when faced with the power of the courtroom dare to speak up for ourselves, even when protesting something as ordinary as a traffic ticket? The mystification process with which courtrooms throughout the ages have enshrouded themselves powerfully shields them from the challenges of defendants, especially those who risk serious jail time or worse. Jesus, just like the once-blind man before the Pharisees, models the behavior expected by Christians when called upon to speak truth to power. Second-century Christian documents are replete with stories of this sort of bold witness, empowered by the advocacy of the Spirit to resist the false power of the world.

And it is precisely at this moment, when Jesus suffers the first physical and socially ostracizing consequence of his plain public speaking, that the story returns us to the fireside where, we are reminded, Peter was "standing and warming himself" (18:25). This time, his challenge comes not from the servant girl alone, but from "them." Just as the once blind man was faced with the anonymous accusations of "them" (9:24ff.), so Peter is confronted with this most fearsome of accusers. The question is exactly the same the second time around, as is Peter's response: "I am not!" Quickly, his karma comes home to roost, as the final question is addressed to him by a slave of the chief priest, "a relative of the one whose ear Peter cut off." His misguided act of militant messianic revolution distinguished him from the crowd of disciples in the garden, allowing for an eyewitness identification of him at the fire. Desperate as he stands surrounded by accusations on all sides, Peter is nothing but denial. He is a caricature of discipleship. With the predicted cock's crow, the lead disciple disappears from the scene, not to reappear until after the first witness to the empty tomb has testified. John's gospel withholds the tearful expression of Peter's bitter regret found in the synoptics (Mk 14:72; Mt 26:75; Lk 22:61). Instead, it allows the scene to close without comment, leaving it to our imaginations to guess how we might react if we stood in Peter's shoes.

"MY REIGN IS NOT OF THIS WORLD" (JOHN 18:28-19:16a)

Not a single word from the mouth of the Judean chief priest is recorded during the preceding interrogation of Jesus. The narrator, as we have seen, focuses attention on Peter's denial and on Jesus' shift of inquiry from himself to that of his disciples. The following scene, however, is of an altogether different character. It contains three interconnected trials:

- Jesus tried by the Roman governor, Pontius Pilate;
- Pilate tried by God's emissary, Jesus;
- The Judeans tried by the Torah under the prosecution of Pilate.

Each "defendant" is allowed to express his own testimony and each prosecutor to ask his own questions. While the chief priest's questions to Jesus were only implicit, Pilate asks *eleven* questions of Jesus and the Judeans. Each of these inquiries allows the respective defendants to reveal their loyalties while they simultaneously challenge readers and listeners to consider their own answers. The heart of the Good Friday drama is found in this courtroom catechism. The character of the church today turns on its responses to these queries.

"What Charge Are You Bringing?" (John 18:28-32)

Before Jesus is brought to the Roman governor, the narrator implicitly notes that the interrogation of Jesus by Caiaphas has been omitted from the story. In 18:24 we were told that Annas had Jesus delivered over to his son-in-law, the official chief priest. Now, in 18:28, we are told simply that Jesus was led away from Caiaphas and toward the praetorium, or governor's palace. What happened between Jesus and Caiaphas? Why does the narrator mention the movement of the prisoner without telling the story? Surely it would be an interesting scene to overhear, as the wily, politically astute Caiaphas finally encounters the Human One face to face.

But the excision of this episode from John's gospel underscores the gospel's sense of how and why Jesus ended up on trial in the Roman court. We recall that the Sanhedrin, led by Caiaphas, has already agreed to condemn Jesus and has already provided its justification for its intended action. Caiaphas has no intention of honestly listening to whatever Jesus might have to say, just as Jesus apparently has no intention of repeating for the chief priest what he has already said openly in synagogue and Temple. Rather than distract our attention with another backroom interrogation of Jesus, the narrator moves on to the more dramatic encounter in which the battle over the meaning of *king* will be fought.

The initial attention in the opening scene is on the politics of place, specifically, the praetorium. The Judeans' concern over ritual impurity is bitterly juxtaposed with their murderous intention. Their fear of physical contact with the pagan palace in light of the impending Passover feast establishes the Torah at the outset as the text from which their own judgment will issue. Neither Jesus nor Pilate is subject to this test. Despite the Judeans' attempt to justify their charge against Jesus under the Torah (19:7), their ultimate appeal will be purely political (19:12). Similarly, Jesus' challenge to Pilate comes not from Torah but from "the truth," the Prologue's own standard of judgment (1:17). From the outset the story makes it clear that "Moses [the Torah] will be [the Judeans'] accuser," just as Jesus had told them (5:45).

The willingness of the Roman procurator to accede to the demands of the Judean purity code by coming out of the praetorium to meet them is a remarkably ahistorical description of the character of Pilate. We should note that the gospel assumes that readers are familiar with Pilate, as he comes onstage unintroduced. The evidence regarding Pilate external to the New Testament suggests a vicious imperial bureaucrat, concerned only with preserving order in the colony under his jurisdiction. The Jewish historian Josephus, writing for a Roman audience, describes a governor perfectly willing to slaughter resisters en masse. The likelihood that such a man would go out of his way to respect local religious customs is remote. What we have instead of a historically accurate description is a carefully crafted characterization that emphasizes *the prearrangement between Jerusalem and Rome to have Jesus executed*. We recall that Judas arrived with the entire cohort of Roman soldiers along with the Temple police. The Sanhedrin has clearly already met with Pilate and obtained his agreement that the death of Jesus is necessary to maintain civil harmony. Pilate's willingness to go out to meet the Judeans is part of the agreement.

In light of this scenario we find that Pilate's questions to the Judeans are not sincere inquiries but rather are part of his plan to belittle the Judeans publicly by reminding them of how dependent they are on Roman cooperation to carry out their scheme. Their responses to him attempt, in turn, to remind Pilate of the political consequences to him of allowing a rabble-rousing revolutionary to remain at large. Their exchange is not unlike a U.S. Senate floor debate on a bill for which the votes have already been counted, but from which political points can still be made by embarrassing the other side "on the record." Both sides know that the outcome is predetermined. What remains to be decided is the outcome of the ongoing jostle for power that is a part of all political action within established state structures.

Thus, Pilate's opening question to the Judeans emphasizes his power over them. They require imperial support to carry out the death sentence in a manner that does not leave them solely responsible for Jesus' execution. Rather than name the real charge—that Jesus is a threat to the Sanhedrin's authority over the people and, therefore, a threat to Pilate's authority as well—they implicitly refer to the prearrangement (18:30). That is, they would never have made a deal with a pagan ruler if they hadn't already agreed that the combined power of Jerusalem and Rome was necessary to get rid of Jesus in a politically expedient manner.

Pilate mocks their holier-than-thou pose by threatening to renege on the deal. If they don't like the "dirtiness" of forming an alliance with Rome, let them carry out the deed themselves! As we have seen, their plea that "it is not lawful for us to kill" is a sham; they have already repeatedly attempted to stone Jesus (8:59, 10:31). Instead, it is a concession to Pilate's necessary role in the conspiracy. If the execution is not to appear to be the action of a lynch mob, it requires imperial sanction. *Lawful* in this context refers not to the requirements of Torah but of Roman colonial authority.

The narrator breaks in on this exchange to express the "heavenly" perspective on these very "earthly" machinations. Beyond the maneuverings of "the world" lie the intentions of God. Crucifixion, despite all appearances to the contrary, is not simply a humiliating act by the empire but is a "lifting up" of the Human One in glory, ordained by the Father (3:14, 8:28, 12:32). It is the second narrative "fulfillment" in the passion narrative of Jesus' word (18:9).

"You're Not a King, Are You?" (John 18:33-38a)

The scene changes as Pilate goes back into the praetorium for his first personal encounter with Jesus. His initial question gets directly to the political heart of the matter: "You are the king of the Judeans?" (18:33). Unlike the chief priest, who was interested in Jesus' disciples, the Roman governor's inquiry is concerned only with Jesus' personal claims. Pilate knows, of course, that Jesus is *not* the colonial puppet monarch. His question expresses his disbelief that this *nobody* is the one who has so aroused the Judean rulers. Further, the suggested object of Jesus' rule mocks the national aspirations of the Sanhedrin. We recall that Nathanael's enthusiastic messianic acclamation of Jesus proclaimed him "king of *Israel*" (1:49). Jesus as the king of *Judea* acknowledges the colonial situation by denying even the imaginative possibility that Jesus' reign could encompass the entire historical patrimony of Palestine. Pilate's sarcastic question reveals his understanding of the dispute as purely internecine; it is a matter of jealous political jousting over who can claim to rule under Roman oversight.

Jesus, however, turns the question back at Pilate. Just as he controlled the interpretation of his arrest and his interrogation at the hand of the chief priest, so too Jesus controls the conversation with the Roman governor. The question underscores Jesus' understanding of the conspiracy between Rome and Jerusalem. He penetrates the official facade and confronts Pilate with his own duplicity, a bold tactic indeed before a heartless imperial authority.

Pilate continues the battle of questions by distancing himself from the dispute but phrasing his inquiry in a manner laced with high irony for readers of John's gospel: "I am not a Judean, am I? *Your* nation and chief priests handed you over to me." Pilate refuses to acknowledge his self-interest in the fate of Jesus, continuing to play the role of the lofty Roman judge. From his perspective, Jesus and the Sanhedrin are on the same side, while he watches their dispute from above. From the gospel's perspective, though, it is Pilate and the Sanhedrin who share an alliance, while Jesus judges them all on behalf of God. Pilate's rhetorical "I am not a Judean, am I?" claims his Roman identity over against Jesus' and the Sanhedrin's shared ethnicity. But as we have seen, *Judean* in the gospel refers not simply to ethnic identity but to theopolitical commitment. A Judean is anyone who benefits from and therefore defends the status quo. Pilate's question is not as rhetorical as he imagines, for to the extent that he becomes a willing accomplice in the Sanhedrin's scheme to preserve the status quo through the death of Jesus, he becomes a Judean, regardless of his Roman citizenship!

His follow-up question to Jesus emphasizes the suspicion that the accused king has engaged in politically subversive action. Pilate does not ask, as did Annas, about Jesus' teaching. Instead, he asks, "What did you *do?*" Jesus responds by answering the governor's first question. His answer is misinterpreted by commentators committed to a spiritualized, politically detached Christianity. Rather than suggesting that Jesus' kingdom is in heaven and therefore that Christians should avoid political involvement, Jesus' answer carefully focuses not on the "otherworldly" *location* of Jesus' kingdom but on its otherworldly *source*.

As we have repeatedly seen, especially in the Last Supper Discourse, "world" is not synonymous with the created earth but with the dominant culture of darkness and violence. Jesus could hardly make this distinction more clear than by his counterfactual suggestion in 18:36b: "*If* my kingdom were of this world, *then* my forces [Greek, *hypēretai*, the same word translated as "police" when referring to the Sanhedrin's forces] would be struggling to keep me from being handed over to the Judeans." That is, Jesus' kingdom is *not* like Caesar's or Herod's; it does not require the violent maintenance of power over others. This does not imply, though, that Jesus reigns only in the afterlife. Rather, it simply denies the similarity of Jesus' reign to kingdoms born of blood, the will of flesh, or the will of a man (1:12) without telling the governor (yet) what that kingdom *is*.

Ironically, Jesus' statement provides further evidence for the truth of Peter's denial of his own discipleship. Peter's attack on the chief priest's slave revealed his own understanding of Jesus' reign as precisely what Jesus now denies. Until Peter and his successors come to understand and embrace this difference, they are not truly following Jesus' way. The irony of centuries of Christian imperialism and repression and persecution of dissenters hardly need be mentioned!

How might these words sound in the ears of Pilate? Just as Nicodemus could not comprehend Jesus' challenge to be born again/from above (3:4, 9), Pilate cannot hear the implications of Jesus' words. All he hears is that Jesus seems to be acknowledging the charge of royal pretension. If Jesus is willing to agree to this, the charade can come to an end and the anticipated execution can take place.

Jesus, however, will not let Pilate out of the situation so easily. His opening words are found in all four gospels: "*You* say!" But the Johannine Jesus adds, "that I am a king," keeping the political question open. His response continues by putting before the Roman governor the challenge his presence in the world has put to all who have heard him speak. Jesus' kingdom is not about maintaining "peace" through violence and exclusion, but about "bearing witness to the truth" (18:37b). It is God's love for the world, which seeks to shed the light of truth in the places of darkness and "foul deeds" in order to save the world from itself (3:16-21). Even Pilate is confronted with the crisis that the Word of God generates by its presence in the world. But rather than formulate the issue in biblical theological terms that the Roman governor cannot possibly understand, Jesus puts the alternative in terms of "being out of truth." We should note that there has been not a word of "God-talk" between Pilate and Jesus. The conversation is purely political; the issue is one of taking sides in the battle for hearts and minds.

Pilate, however, is a pragmatist. His position of authority has not come from allegiance to principles but from effective execution of his duty to maintain imperial order. His famous rejoinder, "What is truth?," expresses his disgust for what he perceives to be abstract philosophical debate. "Truth," as every politician knows, is a relative phenomenon. Only dreamers and fanatics deal in such abstractions. The "real world" cannot be bothered with such arguments. That Pilate does not believe the question is susceptible to a meaningful answer is indicated by his unwillingness to wait to hear if Jesus will answer. With the governor's refusal to engage the question of truth, the first phase of the trial comes to a close, and Pilate goes back outside to issue his verdict.

"I Find No Cause in Him" (John 18:38b-40)

We can only imagine the impatience of the Judeans waiting on the outside while Pilate is interrogating the prisoner. They know that the confrontation inside cannot lead to any real discussion, the fate of the would-be messiah having already been decided.

Pilate is toying with the "king," just as he toyed with the Sanhedrin before entering the praetorium.

But to their surprise, he comes out to them with an unexpected "verdict": "I find no cause in him" (18:38). John's gospel will have Pilate express this conclusion three times before, in the end, he turns Jesus over to be crucified. For now, the first statement can only infuriate the Judeans, who must resent this sarcastic poking at their dependence on his finding of "guilty." He has agreed to join their conspiracy, but he will not do their will until he has extracted a terrible "confession" from them.

Before they can react, he makes them a counteroffer, based on their supposed custom of having a prisoner released for Passover. Historically, there is no evidence for such a custom, nor would such a practice make sense in light of Pilate's record of cruelty. All the canonical gospels tell the story of the preference of the opponents for Barabbas over Jesus, but only John's gospel attributes the offer to Pilate's respect for a Judean custom (cf. Mk 15:8, suggesting it is *Pilate's* custom). Pilate's offer of the release of Jesus again puts the murderous intention back on the Judeans.

The wording of the offer and their response, though, contains a subtle irony that would not have been lost on early readers. Pilate's offer is to release not "Jesus" but "the king of the Judeans." We all assume, of course, that this title refers to Jesus, the one with whom Pilate has been discussing the nature of kingship. But in light of the Judeans' response, another implication can be found. They know before we do that *another* prisoner is in the dock: Barabbas, whom the narrator describes as a "bandit," one of the Robin Hood-like resisters who disrupted the status quo by stealing from the rich on behalf of the village masses. Yet their answer is highly ambiguous: is "this one" whose release they reject the one they consider "king of the Judeans," that is, "don't release the king of the Judeans, but release Barabbas"? Or does their answer suggest that "the king of the Judeans" is not "this one" but is Barabbas?

The intentionality of this ambiguity gains a measure of indirect support when we compare the way the synoptic gospels tell the story of the proposed release of Barabbas. In both Mark and Matthew the narrators tell us about the fact of Barabbas before Pilate makes his offer (Mk 15:7; Mt 27:16). And in both, Pilate's offer is in the form of a direct choice rather than the more open-ended version found in John's gospel. The effect is to suggest, in typical Johannine fashion, that the Judeans unintentionally speak the truth: Barabbas, the violent dissenter who intends to undermine the Sanhedrin's maintenance of its elite economic power over the peasant majority, is more the king of the Judeans than is Jesus, whose kingdom is "not from here."

In any event, the Judeans' preference for the release of a bandit over the Messiah puts another point on Pilate's side of the scorecard. His mockery of them continues unabated, as he turns away from the Judeans to brandish a bit of imperial authority for the rejected prisoner.

The Mock Enthronement of the King (John 19:1-3)

The centerpiece of the multiple trials contained in this current episode is found in the mocking of the royal Jesus by the representatives of the empire. The scene begins with the shocking move by Pilate to have Jesus scourged, a terrible punishment for one in whom he has just found "no cause." If we had not heard the story so many times before, how might we react to this sudden display of apparently arbitrary cruelty?

The particular term used in the gospel refers to the torture of a prisoner with a barbed whip in preparation for execution. The act reveals Pilate's admission that the rhetorical exchange is a facade. In the end he will comply with his end of the bargain and put Jesus to death.

In the meantime, he allows his minions to engage in the traditional ritual mocking of royal pretenders. It was apparently a common practice in the Roman empire ritually to humiliate such political prisoners. The specifics of the mocking are intimately connected with Rome's imperial ideology. The crown of thorns imitates Caesar's laurel wreath, while the purple robe stands in for the royal cloak. The irony of Rome's "recognition" of Jesus' kingship in the face of the Judean rejection of it underscores the gospel's political import: Jesus is not simply a "religious" figure, but one to whom even "pagan" rulers must respond.

The sham monarchical coronation is followed by two particular acts of humiliation by the soldiers. They greet Jesus with a sarcastic proclamation of his title as "king of the Judeans" and dishonor him with slaps to the face. The slaps from Rome's soldiers are precisely parallel to the slap from the chief priest's officer (18:22, 19:3). Jesus has been ritually shamed by both Temple and empire.

As the centerpiece of the entire episode, the royal mocking of Jesus holds before the church the image of *itself* as mocked and rejected by the world. *This* is the way you will be treated if you follow Jesus, says John's gospel. To the extent that the powers of the world offer the hand of friendship to the church rather than a slap in the face, *we* have allowed ourselves to betray this central vision of the passion. When the powers are confronted directly with truth, they will respond by ritually marginalizing the messenger rather than becoming "children of God." This is precisely the import of the gospel's quotation of Isaiah at the summary conclusion of the Book of Signs: the world cannot believe because it has what some have called "Pharaoh's disease," a hardness of heart and blindness of eye that prevents healing (12:40; cf. Mk 8:17-18).

This central image challenges us to rethink our attitude toward those who bear messages we would rather not hear. Why must social justice advocates be so "strident," so "hostile," so "unbending" in their convictions about the need for social change, we ask. Can't we work with rather than against the politicians of church and state? Can't we build relationships rather than simply put the truth "in their face"? These questions haunt those in our culture who are learning to see the truth about who we are. We would like to get along, to be liked, to work gradually, incrementally, to build coalitions among church, business, and government representatives. Armed with our liberal theory of progressive change, we believe that this is more effective than simply stating the truth and letting the chips fall where they may. The picture of Jesus, the king, mocked by both church and state demolishes this liberal illusion. The empire will never be changed incrementally. It will continue to be empire until its dying day, a time the New Testament consistently predicts is coming (e.g., Mk 13:1-2; Jn 16:11; Rv 18). The only Christian response is to continue to speak the truth with love, willing to accept the world's violence and hatred rather than to inflict more violence. Jesus, the mocked king, stands silent before his persecutors, providing a noble example for all his followers to imitate (13:15).

"Behold! The Human!" (John 19:4-8)

Having allowed his underlings to complete their abuse of Jesus, Pilate returns to the Judeans, this time with the mocked king in tow. He intones his second recitation of the verdict of "no cause," as he presents the bloody and beaten Messiah to "his people." The narrator emphasizes, however, that Jesus exits the praetorium of his own volition, reminding us of the divine hand that guides even this dark and frightening passage.

Pilate's proclamation of Jesus as "the human!" allows this off-stage control to reveal itself. The governor's words, almost meaningless from a Roman perspective, invite the Judeans to recall their own messianic hopes:

> And you shall take silver and gold, and make crowns, and you shall put them on the head of Joshua [Jesus], the son of Jehozadak the high priest; and you shall say to him, "Thus says the Lord Almighty, 'Behold the man, whose name is The Branch, and he shall spring up from his stem and build the house of the Lord. And he shall receive power, and shall sit and rule upon his throne'"(Zec 6:11-13).

A humiliated victim of the empire is hardly the fulfillment of the Judean hopes, however. Rather than remembering their scripture, they call on the governor to perform a peculiarly Roman form of torturous execution: crucifixion. In contrast with the synoptic gospels which portray the crowd joining in the call for crucifixion (Mt 27:20-22; Mk 15:11-13; Lk 23:13-21), John's gospel limits the terrible indictment to Pilate's co-conspirators, the chief priests and their police. It is the first mention of this form of execution in the gospel, Jesus having spoken metaphorically of being "lifted up." It comes here as a lightning bolt in the night, an awful acknowledgment of the foul deeds done in darkness of which the narrator warned us after the encounter between Jesus and Nicodemus (3:19-20).

Lest we think that this open "confession" of their desired outcome would bring the drama to an end, Pilate taunts them once more with his third finding of "no cause." What is Pilate after? Is this simply a tyrant having as much "fun" as possible exercising his imperially derivative authority? Or is there something specific he is seeking in his refusal to get the matter over with?

Whatever may be in Pilate's heart when he offers to let the Judeans crucify Jesus themselves, he is clearly taken aback by their answer. We remember that upon Pilate's first offer to return the matter to the Judeans for judgment (18:31), they simply disavowed the "lawfulness" of their putting someone to death, having previously refused to be publicly specific in naming the charge against the prisoner (18:30). Now they again claim the Law, not as an obstacle to death but as the reason for the requirement of death. They add to this by laying one of their cards down on the table: the charge is not the political one of claiming kingship, but the religious one of "making himself God's son" (19:7).

The confident political operator suddenly becomes "fearful" at the words of the chief priests. He was fully at home in the world of power politics, but the religious realm is outside his ken. We might wonder why someone with the Roman pantheon and cultic worship of the emperor behind him would be frightened by this puny colony's internal theological squabbling. Perhaps he hears in the accusation an echo of the Roman "divine man" mythology, the story of gifted individuals who have been blessed by the gods with special powers. If this is what the Judeans' words mean to Pilate, he may well be nervous about having just beaten and mocked a person favored by the gods. This fear drives the governor to a final confrontation with Jesus, this time stripped of his control.

"WHERE ARE YOU FROM?" (JOHN 19:9-11)

Pilate had no need, of course, to retreat to his private sanctum in order to interview Jesus. They both stood outside together in view of those urging the death penalty. But his fear leads him to seek a quiet space, a place alone with this mysterious prisoner. His question to Jesus completely changes the terms of debate. From kingship, Pilate moves to origins. Could it be that Jesus is truly a messenger from the gods?

Surprisingly, Jesus refuses to answer. It is now the procurator who is on the run, while Jesus looks on with royal detachment. It is not that Jesus has no concern for Pilate's query; he has consistently proclaimed his "where from" throughout the gospel (e.g., 3:13, 6:38, 7:29, 8:23). Rather, he knows that Pilate's question continues to assume the "worldly" premise that is not open to the truth of the matter, as revealed by Pilate's next statement.

Typically, the political bully reverts to form in the face of a silent prisoner. If he won't speak, shake a cross at him! It is precisely for this reason that Jesus refused to answer the "where from" question. Pilate is looking for information, material he can use to consolidate his own position. If Jesus truly is a "divine man," than perhaps he can be of use to the procurator. But Jesus will not participate in these games. Instead, he reveals the deeper truth of "authority" to the imperial governor: all authority is controlled "from above." What appears from the worldly perspective to be the will of the emperor is revealed from a heavenly vantage point to be the will of God. Jesus' impending death appears to be the successful end of the conspiracy of evil, but is in fact the coronation of the king.

And with the shift from political to religious conversation, Jesus introduces a theme that would probably make little sense to Pilate: the question of "the greater sin." Just as "sin remains" on the Pharisees "with him" who claimed to see (9:41) but refused to act in accordance with their vision, so now the harsh judgment is reserved for Judas, the betrayer. Pilate is simply a tool, a bureaucrat carrying out orders. Such behavior is not innocent; Jesus does not absolve Pilate of guilt but rather emphasizes where the *greater* guilt lies.

The tables have been completely turned. It is now Jesus who acts as judge, issuing verdicts against his enemies. Pilate has given up the pretense of power. The fun and games are over. He may not understand "truth" or Jesus' mysterious reference to power "from above," but he has heard enough to change his mind about sharing responsibility for Jesus' death. Better to just let him go than take a chance on arousing the wrath of the gods!

"We Have No King but Caesar!" (John 19:12-16a)

The Judeans can see that Pilate is beginning to back down. The outside/inside wall breaks down as the Judeans' shouts penetrate the praetorium. The Judeans pull their own trump card against their reluctant partner, playing the kind of hardball that politicians throughout the ages immediately understand. They withdraw the theological language in favor of the rhetoric of raw power politics. If Pilate releases Jesus, he is "no 'friend of Caesar,' for everyone making himself king speaks against Caesar" (19:12). To be a "friend of Caesar" is to be a political insider in good standing. The use of the term *friend*, is, of course, blatantly euphemistic in the mouths of the Judeans, and ironic in the gospel narrative. From the Judeans' perspective, it marks not a bond of affection but simply a political alliance. The Judeans' words threaten Pilate with loss of his career ladder. A negative report from the provinces could work against a colonial procurator. His primary job is to maintain order. The failure to control a would-be king would be a sign of his inability to carry out his function. The Judeans have pressed on Pilate's jugular.

Pilate knows it. He sweeps his momentary fears aside with this dousing from the bucket of realpolitik and brings Jesus back outside. Pilate takes a place on the seat of ritual public judgment, to which the narrator adds a translation note. The governor's response to the threat of political reprisal is to bring the Judeans' role in the conspiracy out into the open. *Gabbatha*, the Hebrew word the narrator provides to interpret "Stone Pavement," refers to one of two possible locations in Jerusalem, both of which were associated with the Judean client-king Herod. We should note that Herod himself is never mentioned in John's gospel. The translation note, however, serves to make it clear that the Roman procurator is publicly implicating those who would turn him in to Caesar. The Judeans will get what they are after, but not before paying a terrible price.

The narrator continues to draw our attention back to the Judean context of the scene by marking the time as well as the place (19:14). It is the sixth hour on Passover preparation day, the moment when the traditional priestly slaughter of the ritual lambs was to begin. The ironies are thick. Jesus, the Lamb of God, is about to be slaughtered as one whose death will save the people (11:50), just as the blood of the original Passover lambs saved the Hebrews from the destroying angel in Egypt. Furthermore, this sixth hour contrasts with the previous sixth hour in the gospel, when Jesus was extending the offer of community membership to the Samaritan woman at the well (4:6). Just as the woman's life was exposed to the light of midday, so the foul deeds of the Judeans can no longer be hidden by the darkness of night (cf. 3:19-20). The trial, which began in the dark, has taken all morning, and it erupts into the light which all the world will see.

Finally, the link between the sixth hour and the slaughter of the lambs subtly underscores the legal hypocrisy of the chief priests. The Torah proscribed that the slaughter was to begin at "evening," but to accommodate the need to kill a huge number of lambs, the scribes over the years had manipulated the law to allow for this noontime start. Just as they twisted the Torah to comply with their human rituals, so they contort it to allow for the "legal" justification of Jesus' death.

With this ritual and symbolic preparation, Pilate makes his official proclamation to the Judeans: "Look at your king!" The empire has not only found Jesus not guilty, but it has formally judged him to be the king whom the Judeans reject. Their repeated cries for crucifixion lead Pilate to push his co-conspirators for one more deadly concession.

The chief priests respond with the most terrible confession imaginable: "We have no king but Caesar!" (19:15). This breathtaking statement repudiates the entire biblical heritage. The priests who would declare the procurator no "friend of Caesar" have committed themselves to exclusive allegiance to the emperor. The betrayal could not possibly be greater. An ancient Passover Hagaddah expresses what they have given up: "From everlasting to everlasting thou art God; beside thee we have no king, redeemer or savior . . . we have no king but thee."

Now Pilate is satisfied. He has won the deadly battle among worldly rulers. Those born of "blood" reach the inevitable conclusion of their debate. Pilate has no further need to harass the Judeans and turns Jesus over for crucifixion. The gospel describes the handing over with an ambiguity that seals the narrative's view that Rome and Jerusalem are equally responsible for Jesus death. The text notes that "he handed him to them to be crucified." To which "them" is the narrator referring? Twice Pilate has offered to turn Jesus over to the Judeans (18:31, 19:6). While the imperial procedure would certainly suggest that "them" refers to the soldiers who will momentarily be named as those who crucified him (19:23), at this point in the story the narrator's wording could be equally suggestive of Pilate's final, successful handing over of Jesus to the Judeans. The effect is to underscore that regardless of who performed the actual deed, the Judeans are ultimately the ones who have demanded this outcome. All that remains is for Jesus to walk the *via crucis* for himself.

"ALL HAS BEEN COMPLETED" (JOHN 19:16b-30)

John's gospel narrates Jesus' crucifixion with an amazing depth of symbolic detail, although only some of these symbols can be considered here. Readers are urged to ponder each word and phrase in light of what has gone before and in light of our own world.

The key to interpreting John's gospel's story of Jesus' crucifixion is to view it "from above" rather than "from below." To Pilate and the Judeans, Jesus' death is a victory for the status quo. Another would-be messiah has been destroyed, saving the people from being led astray. Rome has reinforced its authority both against rabble-rousers and against the Judean priests. To Jesus' followers—who are, for the moment, nowhere to be seen— the crucifixion of their Lord seems the worst possible defeat. Rather than rising in triumphant glory against the bad shepherds, Jesus has become a lamb led to slaughter.

The gospel's goal is to reverse this judgment by leading us to read the story as one glowing with the glory of God. It is not the death of an outlaw that is being dramatized but the enthronement of a king, one whose reign is "not of this world." The characterization of Jesus at and on the cross in John's gospel could hardly be more different from the synoptic portrayal. Where Mark shows readers a lonely messiah identified with Isaiah's picture of the Suffering Servant, John reveals a glorious Son of God in all his majesty. Mark's Jesus evokes empathy and identification; John's Jesus calls for worship and obedience.

We must remember that this contrast stems from the situation in which the gospel was written. During Mark's pre-70 C.E. period, the social struggle involved whether the Jerusalem Temple system could survive and, if so, should be respected and obeyed. But during John's period, a generation later, the Temple issue was moot because of its intervening destruction by Rome. Instead, the gospel sought to strengthen disciples against ridicule, rejection, and persecution by those who saw Jesus as the worst sort of false prophet. Its portrayal of Jesus as glorious king may not generate sympathetic feelings, but it does hope to induce awe and respect for the authority of the One sent by God to speak truth to the world. As Jesus told the community gathered at the Last Supper, after his death the Paraclete will "convict" the world of its sin and injustice (16:8-11). For now, the gospel urges us to stand as silent witnesses to the royal enthronement of Jesus the king.

The first invitation to engage this interpretative battle comes with the Judeans' protest over Pilate's words above the cross (19:19-21). The procurator orders to be written, in all the languages of "the [local] world," "Jesus the Nazarene, the king of the Judeans." What he proclaimed from the judgment seat is now preserved in writing for all to see. This final "mistake" cannot be left unchallenged, as the Judeans propose a redaction, telling Pilate to write: "That one said, 'I am king of the Judeans.'" Of course, Jesus never made such a claim; the Judeans openly seek the falsification of the record, a tradition long followed by worldly rulers seeking to justify their homicidal impulses. Pilate, however, refuses, having had enough arguments with the Judeans for one day. Pilate's writing is an act of cosmic truth-telling by the one who disclaimed knowledge of truth. And at the same time, it is an ironic confirmation of Jesus' response to Pilate's inquiry about Jesus' kingship, "You have said it" (18:37).

With the final exchange between Rome and Jerusalem complete, the narrative moves on to present us with the crucifixion itself. The soldiers, in fulfillment of scripture (Ps 22:18), cast lots for Jesus' inner garment, after tearing his outer garment into four pieces. Symbolically, the contrast underscores the distinction between the destruction of Jesus' body and the unity of his spirit. The outer garment can be destroyed, but the inner one (a mere undershirt to the soldiers), is described as woven "from above." It is the same word used during Jesus' conversation with Nicodemus about being "born again/from above," repeated during Jesus' discussion with Pilate about authority (3:3, 7; 19:11). Just as those born of the ways of the world cannot understand Jesus' discourse about God, neither can Rome's minions do other than unconsciously fulfill scripture.

Furthermore, in describing the garment as "woven" as a "whole" (19:23) the narrator evokes scriptural descriptions of the high priest's own garment (LXX: Ex 28:6, 27). Jesus is the priest-king, the one whose rule begins with the offering of his own body as the lamb that takes away sin.

The world's responses to Jesus' impending death are now complete. The text turns to the responses of his community, beginning with the linking of the women with the Beloved Disciple. Only John's gospel records someone present at the foot of the cross besides the women. The narrative brings forward the special member of the discipleship community with Jesus' mother, who has been absent since the Cana story in chapter 2. When we read carefully, we find that the gospel forgoes the connection between Jesus and "his" mother to describe the more ambiguous yet seemingly universal presence of "the" mother (twice in 19:26). She is presented to the Beloved Disciple as "woman," and commanded to "see your son." In parallel fashion, Jesus speaks to the Beloved Disciple with the command, "see your mother." The symbolic meaning of this new family has generated much scholarly commentary because of the many levels at which the scene can be read. Does the mother represent Eve, the "mother of all the living" (Gn 3:20), who is now redeemed by inclusion in the discipleship community? Or is she a symbol of Israel's past tradition, joined with the future Christian story? The deliberate ambiguity of the description leaves us to meditate on how the church that is about to be born will be nurtured by the life-giving inheritance of the past, in contrast with the deadly machinations of the official religion and its representatives.

One might pause here to note that the Beloved Disciple's presence at the cross also implicitly draws our attention to the absence of the other disciples, and in particular, the absence of Simon Peter. In light of the back-and-forth between these two after Easter day has dawned, the gospel's inclusion of one and exclusion of the other from this moment of inheritance will provide an important clue to the narrative's attitude regarding leadership in the church. But for the moment, the gospel's silence regarding the whereabouts of Peter provides another reminder of the price of betrayal.

With the new union between the mother and the favored disciple established, Jesus' mission is complete. All that remains is further fulfillment of scripture, as the gospel again subverts the apparent meaning of Jesus' dying words as he expresses his thirst. He is provided with sour wine, a cheap beverage drunk by soldiers, which would only have prolonged the agony of crucifixion. Yet the offer and its acceptance act out a passage from a psalm previously found in the gospel, Psalm 69. At the Temple, Jesus' expulsion of the money changers and cattle was interpreted (later) by his disciples as in fulfillment of Psalm 69:9: "Zeal for your house will consume me" (2:17). Now it is 69:21 that is recalled: "They gave me vinegar to drink." The repeated fulfillment of scripture at this hour of the apparent triumph of darkness continues to provide hope for discouraged disciples. It offers an invitation to read not only this scene but all of life differently, in the light of God's will expressed in the story. For Christians with eyes to see, there is always the opportunity to look behind the official story—"this one said, 'I am the king of the Judeans'"—to find the deeper meaning—this one is God's beloved son, whose life and death give new meaning to the ancient traditions.

THE CHURCH IS BORN FROM BLOOD AND WATER (JOHN 19:31-42)

Just at this moment of exhortation to faith, the narrator takes us back to the maneuvers of Jesus' opponents. The Judeans hope to seal their hypocritical allegiance to the Torah by gaining assurance that the evidence of their crime can be removed from public sight before Passover begins. They go back to Pilate once more to ask that he speed up the execution a bit by ordering the breaking of Jesus' legs. Perhaps surprisingly, the procurator complies with this request and sends the soldiers out on their last mission of the day to Golgotha.

We ought now to be prepared to see the world's actions reinterpreted in light of scripture. The soldiers come to Jesus after breaking the bones of his crucified neighbors and find Jesus already dead. But in a gesture rich with irony, a soldier stabs the dead man anyway. The act appears to be the final blow of Rome, signaling the success of the conspiracy against the self-proclaimed king. Immediately this conclusion is subverted in a remarkable flow of blood and water from Jesus' "side." What can be the meaning of this flow, which the narrator emphasizes with the account of the truthfulness of the eyewitness's testimony?

The scene is incomprehensible in a manner consistent with the gospel's goals unless one looks deep into the text for fulfillment of scripture, both old and new. The word to describe the target of the sword thrust (19:34, Greek, *pleuran*) is one not found elsewhere in the New Testament, but it was used in an ancient story from Hebrew scripture. When God found that the newly created "earth creature" (Hebrew, *adam*) was still lonely, God made a partner from the creature's "side," usually translated, "rib." That is, the "side" is the place from which new life can flow, with God's help, from someone without female reproductive organs. The gospel is calling our attention to the fact that with Jesus' death something new can come to be.

It is the image of blood and water that completes this birth imagery. Where else but in childbirth do humans experience such a flow? The image of birth out of agony has been presented previously in the gospel, when Jesus described the emotional state of the disciples upon the eve of his death (16:21). But the birthing pain will be replaced by the joy of new life, a new life that the gospel has told us will come with the gift of the Paraclete, the Spirit which can only come to be with Jesus' departure (14:17-18, 16:12-14). This linkage calls us back to Jesus' proclamation inviting all who "thirst" to come to him to receive living water, which the narrator interpreted as the Spirit, which will flow from the "belly," translating a Greek word used for uterus when describing the process of birth (7:37-39). All of these symbols combine to suggest to those reading "from above" that the final blow from the empire is what gives birth to the Spirit, which will in turn animate the church about to be born, the community that will grow from the family established at the foot of the cross (cf. 1 Jn 5:5-8).

The narrator provides two explicit fulfillment quotations to get readers in the correct reading mode. The first quotation is a conflation of two different texts, expressing two distinct themes. First is the Passover command about how to prepare the lamb: "a bone of it you shall not break" (Ex 12:46). The second is a prayer for God's protection of the just: "he keeps all their bones; not one of them shall be broken" (Ps 34:20). As we can see, the narrator has tapped into our previous association between Jesus' crucifixion and the sacrifice of the Passover lamb to suggest the first text, but has also used the precise wording of the psalm to lead us to see how Jesus' death fulfills both themes: he is the new paschal sacrifice of whose flesh the people will eat, and also the Just One whom the Lord has protected.

The second fulfillment quotation is from Zechariah 12:10, although interestingly, from the Hebrew rather than the Septuagint version:

> And I will pour out a spirit of compassion and supplication on the house of David and the inhabitants of Jerusalem, so that, when they look on the one whom they have pierced, they shall mourn for him, as one mourns for an only child, and weep bitterly over him, as one weeps over a firstborn.

It is an eschatological passage of God's justice against the bad shepherds of Jerusalem. Thus, with these two fulfillment quotations, the narrator has linked Jesus' death both to the purifying sacrifice of the innocent lamb and God's eventual justice against those who have misled the people for so long. Those who "look on" will be those who have done the piercing, that is, the Roman empire, which will eventually be besieged by Christians witnessing unto death about their faith in the Crucified One. However, we cannot see this fulfillment as directed exclusively against the empire. The Judeans, too, will look on Jesus, as the discipleship community finds its new place apart from the synagogue, and they will wonder just who this one was whom they sent to an apparently ignoble death.

Having established the "victory" of God in the face of the world's opposition, the gospel returns us one last time to the acts of the Judeans. At this late date a new character is introduced to join one known to us previously. Joseph of Arimathea is described as "a disciple of Jesus, but in secret for fear of the Judeans" (19:38). This introduction should warn us against trusting his pious acts, for he falls directly into the category of semi-disciples for whom the gospel saves its greatest wrath (9:41, 12:42-43). Yet we cannot deny the boldness of his approach to Pilate to seek possession of Jesus' dead body, a request which is granted. Joseph's successful access to the procurator suggests that he is a member of the Jerusalem elite, one not unlike the disciple who attempted to gain access to the high priest's house for Peter (18:16).

To risk so quickly being associated with an executed criminal would be a huge gamble. Furthermore, his physical attention to a dead body would cause him to contract ritual impurity that would prevent his participation in the Passover for a month (Nm 9:10-12). Joseph may not yet have confessed his discipleship allegiance publicly, but his actions now threaten to break the silence.

Just at this moment Joseph is joined by Nicodemus, his fellow secret disciple. Together, they follow the Judean burial ethos by wrapping the body in aromatic spices and binding it in bandages (19:40). The gospel precedes the description of their pious act by provided a tragicomic note about the quantity of material with which they have come: "a roll of myrrh and aloes weighing a hundred pounds" (19:39). How did they drag this huge bag of spices to Golgotha? Was it waiting in the wings, having been reserved ahead of time for the inevitable result of the priestly conspiracy with Rome? If so, the "royal" burial is sharply double-edged: if Joseph and Nicodemus were so willing to act boldly and extravagantly upon the dead body of Jesus, why weren't they willing to speak up among their peers to prevent his death in the first place? It is the nature of their brand of half-hearted loyalty to offer homage publicly only after their hero has become a martyr figure. Their act is not unlike U.S. government officials who reviled Martin Luther King, Jr., while he was protesting racism and the Vietnam War, which was an expression of that racism, but build monuments and create holidays in his name now that he is safely dead and buried. Similarly, how many holy Christians have barely escaped the heretic's stake only to be later canonized? The synoptic Jesus himself proclaims the hypocrisy of such worship (Mt 23:29-35; Lk 11:47-51). John's gospel leaves it to readers and listeners to interpret the scene. The plethora of modern commentary defending Joseph and Nicodemus as true disciples only reveals the degree to which many Christians unconsciously identify with their style of discipleship.

Furthermore, their anointing of the body ignores the previous anointing performed by Mary of Bethany, which Jesus expressly interpreted as "in view of my burial" (12:7). Either the men have not accepted as "legal" the woman's act, or their attempt to keep their discipleship secret prevented them from seeing or hearing about it! For this most egalitarian of gospels, such a potentially patriarchal act should gain little respect from the discipleship community.

Their attempt to maintain loyalty both to Jesus and to the tradition of the Judeans is once more pointed out with the notation that they put Jesus' body in a nearby tomb because the Passover preparation required the cessation of work (19:42). The gospel traps Joseph and Nicodemus in the amber of ambiguity, holding up their example to the church as one that, though well-intentioned, only ends up burying Jesus out of public view. They have reversed Jesus' act of liberation to Lazarus, who was ordered by Jesus to be unbound and set free (11:44). Their binding and anointing is intended to keep Jesus in the ground for a long time, safe from the dishonor of decay. That is as far as their discipleship imagination can go, which, of course, leaves them in the same place theologically as Jesus' more open disciples. The whole world expects Jesus to remain buried, removed, another story with a tragic ending. And that is the way the story appears to end. For a while, anyway.

—PREACHING AND REFLECTION IDEAS—

Preaching Themes

1. Reflect on Good Friday as a story not only about Jesus' fate but about the discipleship of those listening to the story being proclaimed. Do we watch from "outside" like Peter, in fear that someone will identify us with the one in the hands of the political powers? Do we have the courage to stand at the foot of the cross with those humiliated by the powers in our own world? Share stories of faithful witnesses, both historical and local, as examples of avoiding the fate of Nicodemus and Joseph of Arimathea.

2. Consider the effect on the world's powers of an individual willing to face persecution and death rather than denying the truth. Use historical examples of persons condemned but later honored for their faithfulness and courage: St. Joan of Arc, St.

Thomas More, Teilhard de Chardin, local persons from the "little tradition" with whom the congregation can identify. Imagine how church members might be able to support one another in taking heroic stands for truth in everyday life, for example, against the abuse of women and children, the vilification of immigrants and other foreigners, the scapegoating of the poor.

3. Reflect on the interpretative battle that rages each day over the meaning of events. Take an example from the current news and show how a "world's eye" perspective might differ from a "God's eye" perspective. Invite people to consider in their own lives how success and failure are matters of interpretation.

4. Consider the difficulty of breaking with one's culturally inherited tradition in the name of the gospel. Reflect on Nicodemus's and Joseph's struggles to leave the Judean ethos behind. What aspects of cultural or church tradition might we be called to leave behind in favor of following God's call to discipleship? How might such a breaking away affect those with whom we share cultural or religious traditions?

Small Group Activities

1. Imagine the trial between Pilate and Jesus taking place in our own social context. Brainstorm about who in our world might play each of the parts in the drama. Act out the drama in this modern context. Reflect on the experience of translating the passion into current terms.

2. Take some quiet time to pray with the passion story, asking each person to name the character in the story with whom he or she can most identify. Invite those who wish to share something about their reflection and why they identified with a particular character.

3. Make a list of all the passages from the Hebrew scriptures that are either quoted or referred to in the passion as being fulfilled. Have individuals in the group look up each passage, and then go around the group reading them. Discuss why the

author of John's gospel might have chosen these particular passages to interpret Jesus' death. How does each person feel about the Jesus found in John's version of the passion?

4. Prepare ahead of time a side-by-side comparison of Mark's and John's passion accounts. Make a list that all can see of all the elements of each passion not found in the other account. When finished, consider the overall differences in portrayal not only of Jesus but also of the other characters described in the two stories. Invite discussion of the passion stories as interpreted narratives seeking to induce discipleship rather than as historical reports simply conveying facts. What does this distinction say about the faith of the church on the eve of Easter?

Reflection Questions

1. *Personal:* How does the passion according to John leave me feeling? How does hearing this story on Good Friday invite me to a deeper commitment to discipleship? Is there a specific part of my life that is challenged by the story this year?

2. *Social and cultural:* How and where is this story relived in our own world today? Consider some specific incident that seems to have parallels with the passion story. How was the incident reported by the media (if it was reported)? Which of the perspectives described in John's story are you encouraged by your culture to identify with: the expediency of the Judeans, the power politics of Pilate, the steadfast courage of Jesus, the cautious risk-taking of Nicodemus and Joseph, the following of orders of the Roman soldiers, the confused witnessing by the women and the Beloved Disciple at the foot of the cross?

3. *Ecclesial:* What does the tradition of reading this story each year say to the church's own role in the world? How does your church respond to challenges to tradition? Consider your own experience, if any, of suggesting changes in church practice.

10

Easter and Beyond

The Birth of the New Community

Can we, after two millennia of Christianity, imagine what it would have been like to experience Jesus' crucifixion and burial without the knowledge that Easter was just over a day away? For many of us, Easter happens "before" Good Friday: our willingness to walk as witnesses to the *via crucis* is grounded in our faith in the Risen One. Certainly the first New Testament writer, the former Pharisee and persecutor of Christians, Paul, came to Christian faith in this order (Acts 9; Gal 1:13ff.). Only the characters named in the gospel accounts were faced with the primordial struggle to trust in God in the face of the apparent victory of the powers of darkness.

As we come to the resurrection stories, then, we cannot easily don the cloak of naivete. The gospel writers knew this reality. None understood it better than the author of John's gospel. The stories that comprise the final two chapters of the gospel form an intricately woven narrative which not only ties together the loose ends of the preceding stories but also becomes a lifeline that links the interior life of the church with its mission to the world.

The common lectionary selects three excerpts from this fabric of faith as gospel readings for Easter and the following two Sundays. While the passages chosen are powerful as free-standing episodes, their removal from the text into which they have been woven can lead readers and hearers to lose the overall thrust of John's theology of resurrection. For example, the Easter Sunday reading tells the story of Mary Magdalene's encounter with the empty tomb, which leads to the comical race between Simon Peter and the Beloved Disciple (20:1-9). The Second Sunday of Easter reading, however, skips over Mary Magdalene's encounter with the Risen Jesus—*the first one in the story*—to narrate Jesus' appearance to the gathered community (20:19-31). This editorial decision cannot help but lead hearers to focus on the experience of *male* disciples, even though the gospel author has carefully structured the story to emphasize the *primal experience of a woman as the first "apostle" of resurrection faith* (20:17-18; cf. 4:28-29). Such a difference in emphasis is crucial in a gospel that has as one of its central tenets of community life the call to establish egalitarian relationships among members regardless of gender, ethnicity, or class status.

Another attempt to tear the seamless garment of the gospel's resurrection stories into pieces comes from scholarly analysis removed from the observation of many readers/hearers but of great influence upon pastoral workers teaching or preaching from the text. The prevalence of historical-critical biblical studies has led to a scholarly consensus that finds the stories contained in John 21 to be an epilogue added at some later date to the "complete" text, which ends at 20:31. There are, however, many problems with this thesis, not the least of which is the total absence of manuscript evidence to support the notion that a complete gospel text without John 21 ever circulated. From a literary and theological standpoint, though, there are many reasons to read the text as we have it as a unit (apart from the story of the woman caught in adultery, John 8:1-11, which the manuscript and linguistic evidence *does* establish clearly as a later insertion).

The lectionary avoids this academic discussion by presenting the passage at the beginning of John 21 on the Third Sunday of Easter which includes the note of narrative continuity at 21:14. Once again, however, the selected passage omits a crucial element of John's story, the final "dispute" over the relationship between the fates of Simon Peter and the Beloved Disciple, as well as the formal conclusion of the gospel (21:20-25). The cumulative effect is to frame the three readings with the experience of Simon Peter, and to marginalize the roles of Mary Magdalene and the Beloved Disciple. As one commentator has noted, the lectionary committee is one of the most powerful forces in the church, because its decisions shape how Christians hear the good news in the primary, liturgical context.

Our challenge, then, is to continue to read the stories as the gospel itself, rather than the lectionary, presents them. Our ideas about the form and purpose of church leadership may be greatly affected by following the resurrection narratives through from beginning to end.

EASTER MORNING: THE UNEXPECTED DISCOVERY OF THE GOOD NEWS (JOHN 20:1-18)

The initial passage comprising 20:1-18 is shaped so that Mary Magdalene's experience "sandwiches" that of the male disciples. Mary moves from personal questioning and experience to service and witness to the community; the male disciples move from individual witness to a retreat "back to their own." The men are at the center, while the women (20:2, plural) "surround" them.

This structure also serves to separate the initial story from the ones that follow. For all four canonical gospels Mary Magdalene's experience is primal, either individually or with other women, over that of the male disciples (Mk 16:1; Mt 28:1; Lk 24:10). Only John's gospel intensifies the drama by wrapping her experience around the mysterious race between Peter and the Beloved Disciple. The result is a message of hope and challenge that overturns the Rome-Jerusalem conspiracy and prepares for the call to the discipleship community to a renewed commitment to faith-filled mission in the world.

In the first verse the gospel draws upon its extended metaphor of light/dark day/night in pinpointing the moment at which Mary Magdalene arrives at the tomb: "the first day of the week . . . early, while there was still darkness." In contrast, Mark's gospel describes it as "very early on the first day of the week . . . when the sun had risen" (Mk 16:2). It is perhaps ironic that for the first gospel Easter comes *after* sunrise, but no actual encounter with the Risen One is ever narrated, while the fourth gospel reports the moment as occurring *before* the darkness has been fully dissipated but goes on to tell of four separate experiences of the

Risen One. Mary's journey in John's gospel is a stumbling in the dark, a ritual journey whose goal will be revealed as obsolete (11:10).

The movement of the tomb-blocking stone, so important to Mark and Matthew, is mentioned in John's gospel only in passing, to draw our attention away from the tomb and toward the question of Jesus' "missing" body. The drama is magnified by the description of Mary's race back to Simon Peter and the Beloved Disciple before the text tells us what Mary saw, if anything, behind the stone. Our initial (naive) expectation might have been that the mere fact of the stone's movement has caused her sudden reaction and departure. It is not until she arrives at her goal that we discover that she has seen enough to conclude that "they have taken away the Lord from the tomb."

The synoptics all report Mary Magdalene coming to the tomb with at least one other woman. John's gospel seems to portray her as going on this journey by herself, then undermines this perception with her statement to the male disciples that "*we* do not know where they have put him." Since no time seems to elapse between her discovery of the moved stone and her race to where the men are, we can only conclude that she was in fact accompanied by other women, but that the narrator has minimized this aspect of the scene in favor of the focus on her personal reaction *on behalf of* the others.

Mary's rash conclusion is interesting in what it says about both the social situation of the gospel and the phenomenology of faith. Who does Mary suspect of grave robbery? Is her concern the commonplace one that thieves burgled the tomb to steal the cloths and other valuables to be found within? Or is she thinking politically in light of Holy Week, suspecting the Judeans of a final act of treachery? In either case her question represents an attitude with which the discipleship community had to deal in coming to the "impossible" alternative explanation of the empty tomb. The "earthly" perspective, the view "from below," sees the absence of Jesus' body as an implication of *crime*. It assumes the tragic ordinary rather than being open to the holy extraordinary. This is the "stumbling at night" of which Jesus warned before raising Lazarus from the dead, the first reaction of all those who for the first time are about to experience God's unbounded power to reopen closed imperial stories.

At the same time, Mary's reference to the missing one contains a note of hope. She refers to Jesus not as Master or Teacher, but as *Lord*, a title that implies Jesus' ongoing sovereignty over Mary's life. And her attitude is not one of total despair, as if the lost body were unrecoverable. Rather, her misguided but persistent goal is to find the place to where the body has been removed (cf. 20:13, 15).

With her announcement, the attention shifts to the men. It is interesting to observe how the gospel "sneaks" Peter back into the story after leaving him at the priestly fire, having (accurately) denied his discipleship. How Simon came to be with the Beloved Disciple a day after Good Friday is omitted, as is any description of the place where Mary finds them. But one thing is clear: they *were* together, and *she knew* where to find them. The fragile community has not been totally demolished by the experience of its Lord's crucifixion. The threads may be thin, but the fabric has not been completely unraveled.

The race to the tomb between Peter and the Beloved Disciple is highly choreographed. The narrator carefully tells us that "they were running together, but the other disciple ran more quickly than Peter and came first to the tomb" (20:4). This is the initial stage in the gospel's theology of reconciliation between two different forms of Christianity that began to emerge in the first post-resurrection decades. Peter, representing "the Twelve" (cf. 6:67ff.), symbolizes the "apostolic" churches, those Christian communities built around the authority of an "original" witness to the resurrection. It is the legitimacy of this basis for church teaching authority that leads Paul so vigorously to claim his own apostolic credentials (e.g., Rom 1:1; 1 Cor 1:1, 15:1-10). By the time of the writing of John's gospel near the end of the first century, the apostolic churches were beginning to re-create a structure of offices within the Christian community that must have seemed to the Johannine community suspiciously like those among the Judeans which Jesus so strongly rejected (e.g., 1 Tm 3; Jn 3:10, 10:12-13).

The alternative to this type of structured institutional religion was the sort of egalitarian, Spirit-driven community for which John's gospel speaks. Just as Jesus challenged Nicodemus, "the teacher of Israel," with the notion that "the spirit blows where it wills" (3:8, 10), so the gospel presents the Beloved Disciple as an alternative to Peter. One speaks as the designee of a group of apostles; the other leans upon the breast of the Lord. More bitingly, one speaks bold promises but ends up a betrayer; the other is silent but stands at the foot of the cross to receive Jesus' mother. What was implicit in earlier scenes now becomes the theme: the Beloved Disciple is John's gospel's way of challenging the emerging hegemony of apostolic church structure.

It is this one who reaches the tomb first. But the dance is not done yet, for the gospel limits his experience at the tomb to a bending over and a looking in, rather than the actual entrance *into* the tomb which the late arriving Peter performs. Simon Peter's act provides him with the identical revelation as that of the Beloved Disciple—"he saw the wrappings"—and more: "and he saw the headcloth not lying with the wrappings but apart, having been rolled up in one place" (20:7). Before Peter can react to this baffling scene, the Beloved Disciple—explicitly noted as having arrived first—makes the next move: entering, seeing, and believing.

But what is it that the Beloved Disciple believed? We cannot be too quick to jump to the conclusion that he believed that Jesus had been raised from the dead, for in the next verse the narrator expressly denies their understanding of this implication of scripture. Furthermore, whatever he believed did not lead him, as it will Mary Magdalene, to proclaim the good news to the community. Instead, the narrator tells us, both the men "went back, therefore, toward themselves." One suggestion is that the Beloved Disciple believed Mary's report that the tomb was empty. Given the overall structural and narrative emphasis in the passage on Mary's movement out of the darkness and into the light, this possibility makes sense out of an otherwise mysterious sequence of narrative signals. In diametric contrast with the usual reading of the lectionary-limited passage as bearing the first expression of resurrection faith in the person of the Beloved Disciple, a reading of the entire episode suggests that the *men's role in the scene is to serve as reliable witnesses to verify Mary's outrageous report!* For a gospel insistent upon the presence of witnesses to its most remarkable stories (e.g., 19:35, 21:24; cf. 5:31ff.), the use of the two (eventually) Christian men most well known to subsequent readers of John's gospel is perfectly fitting.

The evidence of the eyes of both Peter and the Beloved Disciple supports Mary's claim that "they" have taken away Jesus' body.

But what of the amazingly tidy treatment of Jesus' facecloth? It is described both as "rolled up" and "apart" from the other wrappings. The symbols of the scene contain all that disciples need to know to conclude that Jesus has not been "removed," but has risen from the dead on his own power. A few highlights will illustrate the depth of the description.

First, the facecloth's treatment refutes Mary's "earthly" explanation. Neither graverobbers nor Judean conspirators would be likely to act so fastidiously upon a specific piece of Jesus' burial cloths. Another angle must be taken to achieve the understanding the Beloved Disciple could not yet reach.

Jesus' facecloth is not the first one in the gospel. Lazarus, upon exiting the tomb, was described as still bearing a cloth across his face, which Jesus ordered those present to remove along with the other burial wrappings (11:44). Thus, the careful removal of Jesus' facecloth suggests that Jesus himself or an agent of God has removed it!

Reaching farther back into the scriptural story, we recall that when Moses returned to the people after his face-to-face encounter with God on Mt. Sinai, he was covered with a face veil (Ex 34:33-35, LXX, same word as Jn 20:7). If the disciples are to experience Jesus after his own face-to-face encounter with God, it will *not* require the mediation of the facecloth, which has been left in the tomb.

Finally, the cloth was placed upon Jesus' face by Nicodemus and Joseph in accordance with the Judean burial ethos (19:40). The apartness of the facecloth suggests that Jesus has broken through this restrictive ethos. The old way, corrupted by the blindness of violence and the pursuit of worldly glory, has been abandoned. Note that it is not Judaism that has been forsaken but the *Judean* tradition in which the message of the ancestors had become bound. Israel's scriptures are being fulfilled through the restoration of the covenant and the conquest of the "bad shepherds." Christians reflecting on the "victory" of Easter need be ever mindful of this distinction, which the gospel itself preserves so carefully, lest the ongoing scandal of Christian anti-Jewishness be perpetuated.

Taken together, then, we find that the scene within the empty tomb has been crafted to enable the men who witness it to make the leap to resurrection faith. Instead, they retreat to their comfort zones, apparently baffled by Mary Magdalene's true story about a missing body.

The male disciples, having performed their role of verifying Mary's report, leave the stage in favor of Mary's return. We are informed at 20:11 that she has herself come again to the mysterious locale, consumed by mournful tears. Her weeping recalls another aspect of the gospel's first resurrection narrative, when Jesus reacted with strong emotions to the weeping outside of Lazarus's tomb (11:33). Her weeping—symbolic of her lack of faith—is noted four times in five verses. Even the vision of angels in white that she apprehends upon gazing into the tomb does not stop her flow of tears.

Nor does the question from the angels deter her from the mission of finding the location of the missing body. It is a remarkable portrayal that omits any mention of a reaction by Mary Magdalene to this spectacular occurrence. The synoptics are unanimous in showing the women at the tomb overwhelmed with emotion at the experience of the messenger(s) from God (Mk 16:5: "astonished"; Mt 28:5: "afraid"; Lk 24:5: "terrified"). In John's gospel not even a vision of angels can break through Mary's grieving.

The angels apparently disappear when Mary "turned into the things behind" and finds Jesus standing there, unidentifiable through her tears. The phrase used to describe her movement is nearly identical to that of the disciples who will no longer walk with Jesus after the conversation about commitment to the eucharistic community (6:66; also, 18:6), with one telling difference that cracks opens the window of hope. Mary is described as "having turned," a key metaphor in the New Testament for the change of heart required to participate in the discipleship journey. The term is repeated in 20:16 when Mary turns once more to recognize the Lord, who has called his sheep by name.

The drama becomes electric as Jesus himself repeats the angelic question about the cause of her weeping, adding to it the quintessential query of discipleship, "Whom are you seeking?" (cf. 1:38; 18:4, 7). The narrator stretches out the scene further by informing us, tragicomically, that Mary imagines the one with whom she is speaking to be "the gardener," a thought that evokes the Song of Songs imagery upon which this scene is constructed (Sg 3:1-4, 4:12). Not one iota deterred from her mission, she accuses the "gardener" of having taken the body, which is, of course, ironically true. Her journey has reached a cul de sac. Only the voice of her Lord can penetrate and invite her to another turning, one which will invite the world also to turn and be healed (Is 6:10; Jn 12:40).

The translation note provided in the narrator's description of her response underscores the contrast between the rejection of the Judean ethos and the preservation of biblical/Jewish tradition. It reminds us that Jesus' first resurrection witness was a Jew, one who perceived no separation between her heritage and her newly born resurrection faith. It was an important reminder for a community struggling against Judean persecution, when scapegoating the scapegoaters is an all too easy reaction. Jesus' mission through death and resurrection was intended to break the cycle of scapegoating. We need not dwell on the terrible irony of Christian persecution of Jews once the balance of power had shifted centuries later.

Jesus' response to her cry of recognition may seem strangely callous. He forbids Mary to continue "clinging," an act which we had not otherwise known she was engaged in. In addition to calling upon the Song of Songs imagery to proclaim the joyful reunion of lover and beloved (Sg 3:4), Jesus' command calls Mary away from christology and toward discipleship. That is, her desire to cling expresses the church's long-felt urge to worship Jesus as a revered icon rather than by imitating his example of how to live life and how to face death (13:15). He directs her away from a closed embrace and toward a mission of witness to Jesus' community.

The sending forth of Mary Magdalene includes the command to carry the message that "I am ascending to my Father and your Father, to my God and your God." The emphasis is upon the equality of relationship between Jesus and God on the one hand, and the disciples and God on the other. They and we are called by the gospel to become "children of God," an authority that generates this awesome status (1:11-13). Jesus' sonship with God is not, in John's gospel's view, unique. It is a status shared by all those who are born of the resurrection faith that dares to reject the world's glory in favor of the glory of God, a glory which finds its apex on the cross, and its confirmation in the resurrection.

The scene ends with Mary Magdalene's expression of the essence of the new community's faith: "I have seen the Lord!" Despite the ongoing struggle to commit, which remains an element of the journey of faith, the joy of recognition of the risen Jesus is an unsurpassable gift. The delicious savor of its first occurrence remains exclusive to Mary Magdalene, whose story is the gift that enables the community to continue.

—PREACHING AND REFLECTION IDEAS—

Preaching Themes

1. Reflect on Mary Magdalene as the first apostle. Imagine what it would have meant in the highly patriarchal culture of the time of John's gospel to portray a woman as the first witness to the resurrection, the first sent out to preach the good news. Compare the role of the Samaritan woman prior to Easter (Jn 4:28-29, 39). Consider examples of other "unlikely" apostles of the good news in our own time, whether women or other "outsiders."

2. Imagine what it would have been like not to expect Easter to come after Good Friday. Share stories of dashed hopes that did not include an expectation of a reversal which eventually did come. Consider both the pure joy and the social courage that would come with such an experience and what it might mean for the church today.

3. Reflect on the experience of "turning around," which reaches its apex at Easter. Consider how this process does not end with the first telling of the story of resurrection but continues throughout the ongoing cycles of death and rebirth in our personal lives, in our society, and in the church.

Small Group Activities

1. Take some quiet time to imagine what was going on in each character's mind and heart as the story unfolds: Peter, who

had abandoned Jesus and denied being a disciple but who some-how returned to the discipleship community; Mary Magdalene, whose commitment to mourning a terrible death temporarily prevented her from being open to the presence of new life; the Beloved Disciple, who had been so intimate with Jesus; the others who wait while Peter and the Beloved Disciple race to the tomb to investigate Mary Magdalene's story. Invite people to share something from their reflection, including which of the characters they might have identified with during their quiet reflection.

2. Invite people to share their oldest memory of coming to faith in the power of life over death. How has that primal story been sustained as a vehicle of hope in the person's life? Close with a ritual that invites new life to come forth, such as giving a gift of seeds or a young plant that will bear flowers or fruit.

3. Compare John's story of Mary Magdalene's encounter with the empty tomb with another gospel's parallel story. Make a list of the details that differ. Consider how the overall thrust of the story is different because of the details. Discuss why John's version "fulfills" themes sounded earlier in the gospel.

Reflection Questions

1. *Personal:* How might my own commitment to mourning the death of a loved one or of a way of living my life have pre-vented me from being open to the possibility of new life emerg-ing from the midst of a tomb that I had no expectation would ever be empty? How might "angels" or the "gardener" (pow-erful or ordinary witnesses) be inviting me to stop crying over what has been lost and come to see what is waiting to be found?

2. *Social and cultural:* How does our world respond to stories that refuse to end the way they're "supposed" to? Consider examples of persons whose lives became more powerful after they died: Anne Frank, St. Thérèse of Lisieux, or local people. What is the difference between "building booths to dead proph-ets" and celebrating the resurrection?

3. *Ecclesial:* What challenges does John's version of the story of Mary Magdalene's witness provide to the church in which we

participate? Similarly, what might the race to the tomb and responses of Peter and the Beloved Disciple say to the church's practice of leadership and authority?

FINDING JESUS IN THE MIDST OF THE COMMUNITY

After the initial experience of resurrection recognition by Mary Magdalene the gospel moves on to a different theme: the experience of the risen Jesus in the midst of the community. The geography of the second resurrection story is totally different from that of the first. In the previous story Mary Magdalene and the two male disciples left their place of safety to journey to encounter the mystery of the empty tomb. With the discovery of the discarded wrappings, the tomb is no longer important. Jesus has broken the bonds of death; he is free to be experienced in the places of ordinary life.

The movement from Easter to the following week in the life of the church follows a similar transition. After focusing intensely on walking with Jesus amid the Palestinian places of Holy Week and through the historical re-membering of the passion, there is often a letdown in the church's energy. All of the liturgical planning and power that goes into Lent and Holy Week cannot be maintained forever! Inevitably, pastors and staff take much-needed vacations, parishioners drift back into the cycle of everyday life, and newly baptized community members feel the enthusiasm and energy that led to Easter's sacraments begin to fade. It is a difficult period for proclaiming the still-powerful stories that are presented to the community for the next two weeks.

As we shall see, this cyclical emotional letdown is not unique to our short-attention-span culture. The gospel story for the Second Sunday of Easter portrays a community that seems already to have forgotten the breakthrough which Jesus achieved. Rather than fearlessly proclaiming the message of Easter to the world, Jesus' disciples are in hiding, still afraid of the power of darkness embodied symbolically in the persons of the Judeans. Whatever immediate reaction they had to Mary Magdalene's witness—none is recorded—after one week they have no clear idea about how to carry out the mission Jesus has given them. It requires a direct encounter with the Risen One to break them—and us—out of our post-Easter doldrums.

The central emphasis at 20:21-23 underscores the post-Easter theme of Spirit-empowered *mission*, the "breathing out" that balances the Last Supper Discourse's theme of "breathing in," that is, strengthening the internal life of the church. But before the community can engage in this mission, it must learn to overcome the fears that keep it behind locked doors.

The story begins with the narrator's time notation that, remarkably, the long Easter day's experience is not yet complete. It is "evening," a time of diminishing light, a transitional period in which, like the dawn of Mary Magdalene's encounter, dark and light struggle. In contrast with dawn, however, evening inevitably gives way to the dominance of night, a time associated in the gospel with betrayal (13:21-30). It is perhaps sadly unsurprising in this context of fading illumination to find the disciples, who have so recently been presented with the incredible good news of Jesus' ongoing life, cowering in fear. We should note that the narrator never says that they are in a "room," but states literally that "the doors having been locked where the disciples were." Given the previous use in the gospel of "door" as a metaphor for Jesus and his capacity for inviting the disciples into a place of safety and community (10:9), we should not be too quick to fill in the "missing" detail. The issue is not so much the disciples' hiddenness behind physical walls and doors but their locked *hearts*, which have not yet grasped the significance of the day's events.

The description of the disciples as in "fear of the Judeans" puts them in some fairly questionable company. We recall that this condition was what prevented the person born blind's parents from testifying to the one who healed their son, as well as Nicodemus's and Joseph of Arimathea's unwillingness to be known publicly as disciples (9:22, 19:38; cf. 7:13, 12:42). Even on Easter evening the disciples have not been freed of this paralysis.

The antidote to this fear is the presence of Jesus in the community. Far too many homilies have focused here on the "miracle" of the risen Jesus apparently passing, ghostlike, through walls. The text, however, says nothing about such a mysterious passage. Rather, it states simply that "Jesus came and stood in their midst" (20:19). The gospel is not interested in conveying the very signs of faith that Jesus does not trust (2:23-24, 4:48). Instead, it invites readers and hearers to be open to the possibility of experiencing the Risen One within the church, despite our fears of what's "out there" in the world waiting to get us. Is not the greater miracle the ability of Jesus to penetrate the locked doors of our terrified hearts rather than mere bricks and mortar? Which message speaks more directly to the needs of the church, both at the time of John's gospel and today? For behind locked doors in "fear of the Judeans" is precisely where the mainstream Christian community finds itself much of the time. We come together in church buildings but keep our faith secret from the world. We celebrate the power of the tradition during Lent and Holy Week within the comfort zone of the faith community, but we shrink in the face of the challenge to bring that tradition into confrontation with the world's darkness. We don't want to be perceived as religious fanatics or radicals, who take their religion "too seriously," even while we struggle to "make it" by the standards of the world. No people has needed the message of this Second Sunday of Easter more desperately than North American Christians at the end of the second millennium. Jesus' presence in the midst of the church is, as one church leader has described it, an *uprising.* It calls those who would be followers of Jesus to put aside "conventional wisdom" and be energized into passionate public witness by the power of the One who could not be bound by death.

The Jesus who stands in the midst of the cowering community begins this conversion process by offering peace, the biblical *shalom* that calls the people to healing and wholeness. Jesus has already told his community that the peace he gives is not the same as that the world provides (14:27). It comes in the midst of persecution, not as a comfortable state of repose (16:33). It does not mean the absence of conflict or suffering, but rather, the centeredness of the community while it experiences the contrasting "peace" offered by the world. The latter peace is the repressed silence and conformity of empire, the *pax Romana* or *pax Sovietica* that contains but does not heal brokenness. In the American imperial setting the world's peace is not maintained through overt threats of death squads or gulag banishment but through the stultifying "freedom" that allows but constantly ridicules and marginalizes dissent. Jesus' peace converts "disciples" into "apostles"; the students who learned from their rabbi are now sent out (Greek, *apostellō*), just as the Father had previously sent Jesus himself.

The transition from community fear to mission is made through the revelation by Jesus of "his hands and his side" (20:20). We recall that Jesus' "side" was the site of the Roman sword thrust that gave birth to the Christian community (19:34). It now draws the disciples' attention to the contrasting realities of imperial violence and biblical *shalom*. In the text the *shalom* "surrounds" the reminder of crucifixion (20:19, 21), just as Jesus' "I AM" surrounded Judas's betrayal (18:5-8). God's power does not eradicate the world's acts of darkness, but "conquers" them by revealing their penultimacy (16:33).

The presentation of Jesus' hands and side leads the disciples to rejoice at "seeing the Lord," putting them finally into the same company as Mary Magdalene. With this recognition, they are prepared to receive the gift that will empower them for their mission. Just as God breathed on a lump of clay to give it life that participates in the divine power (Gn 2:7), so now Jesus breathes on his newly born community, inviting them to "receive the holy spirit." It is the very spirit Jesus invited those gathered at Tabernacles to receive in the form of "living water," a flow that comes from the core of Jesus' being (7:37-39, 19:34). It is what will enable the community to go back over its experience and reinterpret all that has happened in light of God's Word, both in the existing biblical tradition and in the new tradition of the gospel itself (2:22, 12:16, 15:20, 16:4).

Upon giving this gift Jesus reminds them of the key to the "success" of both community life and mission: the power to forgive sins. In John's gospel this power does not come as a grant to Peter on behalf of the apostolic church leadership as it does in Matthew (Mt 16:19, 18:18-22), but as a "fact" of the community's common life of faith. The contrast may well be another stroke in John's gospel's "rewriting" of the apostolic ecclesiology that was taking shape late in the first century. Jesus' statement is not the authorization of power in the church but of the re-placement of forgiveness from "heaven" to the community itself. Furthermore, it reminds the disciples and us of the essential link between the willingness to let go (the literal meaning of the Greek word translated as "forgive") and the ability to be at peace. To hold on to the sins of others is to allow a sore to fester in the body; to let go is to allow healing to take place. Unless the church can practice this discipline, its ability to persevere in its mission to a world filled with hatred and violence will be sharply curtailed.

Just when it might seem that the scene is complete, the narrator introduces a new theme. Thomas, "one of the Twelve," was apart from the group when Jesus came (20:24). The language suggests not only that Thomas was physically absent, but that there is a serious question about his solidarity with the community in the face of his experience of Jesus' crucifixion. We recall that Thomas was the one who previously suggested to his fellow disciples that they should go "die with him" when he returned to Judea to be with Lazarus's family (11:16). Perhaps a part of Thomas has indeed died with Jesus and has not yet been raised from that death, for the narrator tells us that Thomas "was not with them." This was the kind of description that expressed both Judas's and Peter's distance from discipleship (18:5, 18). Now it is Thomas's turn to confront his own doubts about Jesus.

He is not completely removed from the community, however, for some time after the initial experience of the presence of Jesus in their midst the other disciples shared their good news with Thomas, using the resurrection formula expressed now for the third time (20:18, 20, 25). Thomas's refusal to share in their joy is adamant and focuses on a need for physical proof. It is a struggle that continues to plague would-be believers centuries later, especially in our scientific age. The notion of a risen Jesus who can be seen by disciples is ephemeral. Can we dare to put our life at risk in public witness on the basis of so slender a reed of hope?

It is Thomas, perhaps more than the others, who understands the implications of accepting the revelation of resurrection. If Jesus is simply dead and buried—another failed messiah who could not overcome the power of Jerusalem and Rome to crush dissent—then Thomas, although certainly disappointed, can go back about the "safe" business of everyday life. But if the word of the others *is* true, and Jesus *is* risen, then his words *must* be obeyed as the very word of God that the gospel claims them (and him) to be. If Jesus is truly risen, then his community cannot avoid its confrontation with the hostile world, cannot deny the call to love one another intimately and fully. It may be just this deep recognition that leads Thomas to his powerful statement of the condition required for his trust in the word of the others.

Although the scene that follows eight days later is focused on the movement of Thomas from doubt to faith, we should note the terrible irony of the situation that the narrator presents. Despite the joyful experience of the Risen One, despite the gifts of peace and of the spirit, the disciples are *still* behind locked doors. What were they doing all week? How difficult it is for the church to be about its mission of bringing love and *shalom* to the threatening world!

For now, though, all attention is on Jesus' encounter with the disbelieving disciple, who is described this time as "with them." Whatever has happened to move Thomas to rejoin the community despite his disbelief is not narrated. But his presence there is the precondition of the fulfillment of his hope. Jesus offers Thomas precisely the physical proof he demanded as he commands Thomas to not "become unbelieving but believing." Thomas stands at the great divide between those who take the risk of trusting in the gospel story and those who do not. His response is absolute: "My Lord and my God!" No longer in need of the physical touch of Jesus—which he apparently does not in fact experience—Thomas can proclaim Jesus as the One in whom he puts his trust.

The specific language of Thomas's confession of faith has powerful political overtones. The phrase "Lord and God" was one claimed by the Roman emperor Domitian, who was in power during the late first century. Just as the Samaritans were able to proclaim Jesus greater than Caesar as "savior of the world" (4:42), so now Thomas announces his loyalty to Jesus over the emperor. Such a confession, made publicly, is precisely what will lead many of Jesus' followers to share his fate, just as Thomas had predicted. Imagine the turmoil if liturgical celebrations contained the confession of Jesus as "my president (or prime minister) and my God"! With Thomas's announcement and its repeated commitment by disciples, the power of the world over the church is broken.

The story concludes with the movement from the experience of Thomas and the first community of faith to the situation of all who follow in their footsteps. The gospel was written for Christians who lived long after the first rumors of resurrection had circulated. It is for all of us that Jesus proclaims the final beatitude of the gospel, the happiness of those "not having seen and having believed" (20:29). We must rely on the report of others rather than the invitation to thrust our hands in the sword and nail prints. We must face the more difficult challenge of casting our lives upon the living waters we inherit from those who have gone before us.

It is precisely with this challenge in mind that the narrator concludes the episode with a summary of all that has been written. The gospel is a collection of "signs," an abridged version of the life of Jesus, compiled for a particular purpose. The narrator leaps out of the third person form to address readers and hearers collectively. It is so that "you" (plural) may believe that Jesus is the Messiah, the son of God, titles previously confessed by Martha of Bethany with an element of ambiguity (11:27). The narrator now clarifies that ambiguity by noting that it is not the acclamation of the titles themselves that is at issue, not a mere verbal declaration of allegiance that is called for. Rather, it is so that "through believing, you may have life in his name." It is an invitation to rise from the death this world imposes on people by its rule of nationalism/patriarchy, violence, and conformity to its will (1:13, 5:21). Birth into the Christian community through baptism and the practice of eucharist gives life in Jesus' name that shines into the darkness of the world but is not overcome by it (6:51ff.; 1:4-5). It is for this purpose that these stories have been told and continue to be told. But the gospel is not complete until the disciples learn more about the implications of this new life.

—PREACHING AND REFLECTION IDEAS—

Preaching Themes

1. Reflect on the emotional letdown that comes after Easter. Like New Year's resolutions, Lenten promises of repentance and recommitment can quickly fade into the background of life "as it is." But Jesus comes again each year at this time to break through the lethargy of our lifestyles and breathes new spirit into our baptismal promises.

2. Consider the "conspiracy" of commitment that comprises the cycle of discipleship. Before we can find the courage to get out

from behind the locked doors, we must be willing to receive the gift of the spirit that breathes new life into us. The Easter season calls not for "trying harder to be good" but for eyes that can see the risen Jesus in our midst despite our fears and limitations.

3. Contrast peace as the absence of war or conflict with the biblical *shalom* Jesus offers his frightened disciples. Link the practice of forgiveness among Christians to the practical presence of *shalom* in the community and in the world.

4. Reflect on Thomas's doubts in terms of commitment to Jesus over commitment to "the emperor." What "proof" do we need to convince us that only God can claim the deepest center of our being? What demands do we make of God before we are willing to proclaim Jesus as "my Lord and my God"?

Small Group Activities

1. Invite people to take some quiet time to consider how they spend the week following Easter. Is it just like any other week? What real and lasting difference does believing that Jesus is risen make in the lives of those gathered in this group? Consider ways in which Jesus might be found in the midst of the group during this session together.

2. Discuss the nature of Thomas's doubts and what they might mean for us today. Do we need physical proof of resurrection in order to change our lives? Do we see commitment to Jesus as conflicting with or consistent with commitment to country?

3. Take some time to consider the places of apostleship in the church today; that is, the places where the Christian community is "sent out" to witness to the world. How has the concept of *mission* changed during your lifetime? Where might you be called to be sent forth? Allow time for each person who wishes to share his or her reflections.

Reflection Questions

1. *Personal:* What "Judeans" do I fear that keep my faith behind locked doors? How do I experience the risen Jesus in my midst beckoning me out into the world?

2. *Social and cultural:* In your local area, what is the wider community's attitude toward public proclamation of faith? Consider not simply obvious examples like street-corner preachers or school prayer, but more subtle situations, like faith-based political involvement or lifestyle choices. What practices allow you to experience the presence of the Holy Spirit empowering you to bring your faith out into the world?

3. *Ecclesial:* What issues lead your church to hide behind locked doors for fear of the reaction of the "Judeans"? How is forgiveness practiced in your faith community: through formal liturgical/sacramental practices, through informal rituals, through personal reconciliation, through concrete acts of reparation, or through other means?

FILLING THE BOAT WITH AN ABUNDANCE OF FISH

The final lectionary reading from John's gospel is the passage 21:1-19, which finds the disciples gathered to go fishing back in Galilee. The designated reading omits the closing verses of the gospel, wherein the relationship between Peter and the Beloved Disciple is clarified and completed. It also tends to merge the mission theme of 21:1-14 with the church leadership theme of 21:15-25.Those whose role it is to teach or preach from the lectionary passage would do well to help their audience to see the way the gospel has divided the chapter differently from those who compiled the lectionary cycle.

Fishing at Night and at Daybreak: The Invitation to Mission (John 21:1-14)

The first two Easter gospel passages spring Jesus' resurrection like a surprise party. Mary Magdalene and those gathered behind the locked doors, along with first-time readers, find each scene unfolding without expectation of Jesus' presence. The final story, though, lets the cat out of the bag right at the start. Why does the narrator "ruin" the surprise so quickly? The answer lies in the differing purposes of the three resurrection stories. While the first two have as their goal the initial establishment of the fact of resurrection and the proclamation "I/We have seen the Lord!," the third story's intent is to convince disciples, then and now, of the radical nature of the commitment required to maintain one's discipleship. The fact of resurrection is now taken for granted, in favor of the "surprise" of the huge catch of fish that awaits.

The scene begins at the Sea of Tiberias in Galilee, a place last visited in John 6. Just as Jesus withdrew from Judea to avoid death threats (10:39-40), so the disciples escape from the site of their fear for a more friendly locale. Unlike Mark and Matthew, though, John's gospel has given no angelic command for them to return to Galilee. Instead, we might imagine the fledgling church struggling to discern what the challenge to be "sent" as Jesus was sent might mean for it.

The list of named disciples introduced is the longest such list in the gospel. It combines uniquely Johannine disciples—Thomas the Twin (but cf. Mk 3:18; Mt 10:3; Lk 6:15) and Nathanael—with uniquely synoptic disciples—the sons of Zebedee—with the disciple common to all canonical gospels—Simon Peter. Conspicuous by his absence is the Beloved Disciple, who does not make his appearance in the story until 21:7, apparently one of the "two other disciples" at the end of the list. The effect of this list is to present a scene that brings together diverse Christian traditions, a "conference" consisting of seven—the number of completion/perfection—representatives of both apostolic and Johannine communities.

Furthermore, each of the individually named disciples has been presented in John's gospel according to the same pattern. Each expressed doubts about willingness to follow Jesus, ended up making a grand "confession," and had that confession rhetorically challenged by Jesus. The scene begins, then, in a context of doubt and faith, with the possibility of Jesus' teaching to challenge disciples to a deeper understanding and commitment.

The action begins with Peter's sudden announcement of his intent to go fishing (cf. Jer 16:16). Is this a symbolic expression of the beginning of the Christian mission or an admission that Peter has not at all understood the implications of his experience of the Risen One and the command to be sent forth as Jesus was sent forth? That is, has Peter "returned to the things behind" (6:66, 20:14) or gone forward to reap the harvest (4:38)?

Whichever it is, the others join him. Peter is the leader whom the others follow. Yet under his leadership in the boat, their night expedition nets nothing. It is one of John's gospel's little ironies: although Galilean fishers often worked at night, nothing good ever happens in the gospel in the dark!

Just as Mary Magdalene moved out of the night and into the break of day to experience the Lord, so too the disciples in the boat find Jesus as the darkness turns back to day. Rather than being "in their midst" as in the previous stories, Jesus is apart from them "on the beach." Whether by physical distance from shore or spiritual distance from discipleship, those in the boat "of course" do not recognize the one who speaks to them from the beach. Again as in the Mary Magdalene encounter, readers are let in on the secret before the characters in the story, to draw our attention to whether and how the disciples can come to share in our joy of recognition.

Jesus addresses those in the boat as "little children," from a Greek word that suggests immaturity, yet with an affectionate overtone. Jesus knows that his newly born community is not yet ready to comprehend the full implications of the call to discipleship, so he gently offers the disciples a lesson that will help their development. The exchange about food makes clear that the disciples on their fishing trip are not yet conscious of its symbolic meaning. They are simply about the process of filling their bellies, just like the crowd that followed Jesus across the sea the first time around (6:26).

Upon following Jesus' instruction to cast their nets on the right side of the boat, they immediately find the net brimming with a "multitude" of fish. The term refers back to the "multitude" gathered at the Temple pool seeking healing. Now the import of the scene begins to be revealed: those in the boat are to gather into the community the multitude in need of the healing the Temple can no longer offer (cf. Hab 1:14-15). The Temple/pool typology is replaced by the boat/sea symbolism. Rejecting the grandiose image of the golden Jerusalem structure, which ended up separating the wealthy from the poor, the elite from the masses, John's gospel pictures the church as a humble fishing boat afloat on the sea.

At this dramatic moment the Beloved Disciple appears and immediately speaks to Peter of his recognition of the Lord. It is the Johannine version of the Lucan road to Emmaus story; as the disciples there "knew" Jesus in the breaking of the bread, so now the disciples know Jesus in the gathering of the fish. But Simon Peter is dependent upon the Beloved Disciple for his testimony. The narrator tells us not that Peter shared in the moment of recognition, but rather that he "heard it was the Lord" (21:7). Throughout their relationship the gospel has portrayed Peter as a step behind the Beloved Disciple (13:23-25, 20:4-8). Now it is the Beloved Disciple who first understands the link between resurrection and mission.

Peter's comical leap into the sea contains many poignant, symbolic details. He "girds" himself with his cloak, just as Jesus had "girded" himself to wash the disciples' feet (13:4). In the next scene Jesus will speak of "girding" in terms of the loss of a certain kind of freedom entailed on the journey of discipleship (21:18). For now, the symbol expresses Peter's acknowledgment of his nakedness before the Lord, which came from the lessons in self-awareness he has experienced since his first refusal of the footwashing itself. It is a nakedness that he is not ready fully to reveal.

The leap into the sea is symbolic of Peter's own baptism. He insisted previously, but improperly, upon having "not my feet only, but my hands and head as well" washed by the Lord (13:9). Now he succeeds in being wholly immersed, while the others join the Lord from within the boat. The separation between the group of disciples and Peter is perhaps also symbolic of the emerging role of Peter as church leader, a role considered in detail in the next scene.

A final reminder of Peter's checkered past is provided by the description of the beach fire as a "charcoal fire," a term used elsewhere in the New Testament only to describe the site of Peter's denial in John's gospel (18:18). Now the nighttime betrayal in the face of priestly authority is transformed into a morning meal provided by the grace of Jesus.

Jesus calls upon them to add to the fish he has provided for them from those they have caught (with his assistance). It is an apt symbol for a gospel that will not allow God's authority to be contained exclusively within religious structures. Just as the spirit blows where it wills, so too some "fish" come to the community through the gathering by the disciples into the boat, and others come "directly" by the work of Jesus himself (cf. 4:38). In the end, all are brought together safely on the shore without the net "having broken" (21:11: Greek, *eschisthē*, from which comes "schism").

The conclusion of the scene shows a seaside eucharistic meal, with the emphasis on the fish, an element in many early Christian eucharists. The mission provides its own nourishment for the discipleship community. The fruit of the disciples' journey into the darkness of the world (symbolized by the darkness below the surface of the sea, cf. Gn 1:2) is the bountiful eucharistic banquet, which includes people of every kind (symbolized by the 153 fish).

The lesson of the scene for those having recently entered the church or those long within is clear. When disciples attempt to focus only on their own needs for comfort and security (the night fishing voyage), their efforts are fruitless. Pursuit of personal security is antithetical to the gospel, as Jesus will make crystal clear to Peter in particular in the next scene. Prayers to Jesus for business success are bound to fail; Jesus is simply not listening to such misguided requests. But once one acknowledges one's emptiness, "failures," and resulting dependence on help from God, a boundless "catch" is available, not for the sake of self-gratification, but for the salvation of the world. That the boat may not be big enough is not reason for a capital campaign to expand the church buildings, but for trust that the "earth" (21:11) is big enough to contain those brought out of the dark chaos and into the light and solidity of dry land. The church's home is not behind locked doors but out in the open, exposed yet safely under the guidance of God's spirit.

The Shepherd Must Be Willing to Lay Down His Life for the Sheep (John 21:15-25)

What remains to be learned is how the church is to go forward in carrying out this mission. The joining of the preceding passage with 21:15-19 in the lectionary reading has the effect once more of placing the focus of the entire reading on Jesus' interaction with Peter. While it is certainly true that the role of Peter is of central importance to all of John 21, the gospel is careful to place that role in relationship with two specific contexts. In 21:1-

14 the question is of the link between Peter and "the disciples" as a whole. Peter goes fishing; the others follow. Peter leaps into the sea; the others follow in the boat. The others disembark onto land; Peter hauls in the full net. The single exception—the recognition of Jesus by the Beloved Disciple and Peter's "hearing" it was the Lord—is easily swallowed up in the broader issue of Peter's overarching leadership. This is all the more the case when the passage is linked with the exchange between Jesus and Peter in 21:15-19.

The rejoining of the latter exchange with what follows in 21:20-25 underscores the gospel's concern with the other context in which the role of Peter is to be considered, specifically, the relationship between Peter and the Beloved Disciple. That is, the lectionary's arrangement places the issue of Peter's shepherding as a *conclusion* to the story of the catch of fish (mission), albeit with an abrupt shift in metaphor from catching fish to feeding/tending lambs/sheep. The gospel, on the other hand, has placed the issue of Peter's shepherding at the *beginning* of the story of the relationship between leadership and martyrdom.

The difference for the church is crucial. The fish-catching mission is portrayed as relatively safe. There is no storm at sea as in the previous crossing (6:16-21). So long as the disciples rely on Jesus' guidance, they are able successfully to gather in the fish and to share their eucharistic breakfast. However, as soon as the issue turns to taking care of the sheep, the themes of death and glory quickly reappear. Suddenly, what Jesus the Good Shepherd said about laying down one's life for the sheep comes charging back into mind (10:15). All the implications of footwashing and the Last Supper Discourse are applicable *now*, as the community is called out from behind the locked doors and into the light of day. The community as a whole is called to love one another to the point of laying down their lives for one another (15:12-14). However, the primary burden of walking with this willingness to lay down life for the sheep falls on those who would be "shepherds." If the church is not to fall back into the errors of the Sanhedrin, it must base its leadership on just this criterion.

However, the gospel passage goes on to show Peter asking specifically about the fate of the Beloved Disciple, whom tradition holds was *not* martyred as was Peter. If the community of John's gospel can accept Peter's (the apostolic churches') leadership only on the ground of his willingness to be martyred, what about the leadership of the Beloved Disciple? Must one die a violent political death in order for one's authority to be respected? Or might there be different calls for different leaders? If so, how can the members of the church know if a particular leader is avoiding the call to martyrdom for the sake of self-preservation or because the leader has been given a different calling by the Holy Spirit?

These questions were central to the struggle in the early churches over how to organize the life and mission of the Christian community. John's gospel was apparently written in part to counteract the emerging sense of "apostolicity" read as teaching authority that stems from one's succession to the office of "apostle." It is the Beloved Disciple—never described as an apostle or as one of the Twelve—who beats Peter to the empty tomb and who recognizes the One who provided the abundant catch of fish. It is the Beloved Disciple who reclines in the privileged position upon the breast of Jesus at the Last Supper and learns the identity of the betrayer on behalf of the community. Indeed, it is explicitly the Beloved Disciple who "is witnessing about these things and the one having written" the gospel, at least in the sense of providing the tradition upon which the narrator's community created the text itself (21:24). Why, then, is Peter the one with whom Jesus converses about shepherding the sheep?

The likely answer lies in the sociology of sects, at least as lived out by the Johannine community. Although scholars disagree about the chronology of composition between the gospel and the first letter of John, most take the position that the letter was written subsequent to the gospel, and that it expresses something of the experience of the community after the gospel was written and began to circulate. If so, then we find a community in disarray shortly after the gospel was written. The letter deals with a terrible split in the community, one that leaves the outsiders (from the perspective of the letter's author) labeled as "antichrists" (1 Jn 2:18). The split came precisely over the issue of speaking love without doing it, that is, practicing what one preaches. The point for our current discussion is simply that in the absence of an authority figure who could lay down the law, the community was faced with the alternative of first exhorting the dissenters to return to the shared vision and, failing that, demonizing the opponent. This wrenching dose of reality threatened to crush altogether the vision of egalitarian, Spirit-driven leadership that could not be contained by office. Might there be another criterion by which the community could select authoritative leaders while rejecting the dangers of hierarchical structures?

This crisis has come to many communities of faith over the centuries, especially those ignited by a vision similar to that of John's gospel. Indeed, it was a similar issue that led Israel to move from a tribal confederation to a monarchy, thus betraying God's exclusive ultimate authority in the community (1 Sm 8). In our time it comes to Christian communities that seek to operate beyond official denominational boundaries, especially those with a vision for world transformation. The fiercer one's commitment to a life-risking agenda, the more central the issue of leadership becomes. Soldiers may follow their commanding officer into battle, but did the disciples follow Thomas when he urged them to go die with Jesus in Jerusalem (11:16)? Communities that refuse to grant authority to particular individuals are extremely vulnerable to the same sort of dissension and internal betrayal that faced the community of 1 John.

These, then, are the issues underlying Jesus' triple question-and-answer with Peter after their seaside breakfast. Jesus' statements are not mere repetition with aesthetic variation; they reveal a progression that responds to the reality of Peter's own responses. The core of the exchange lies in the different terms used in Jesus' first two questions and Peter's answers. Jesus seeks Peter's commitment to *agapaō*, the self-sacrificing love that marks the true shepherd. However, Peter answers in terms of *phileō*, the respectable but narrower sense of friendship-affection. Jesus' sense of love is used over thirty times in the Last Supper Discourse alone, nearly half of all the occurrences in the four gospels combined. It is the central discipleship virtue, and Peter cannot muster either the understanding to know that there is a difference between the question and his answer or the courage to match Jesus' question if he does understand. In the final exchange Jesus reduces the demand to what Peter is able to produce, changing the question from *agapaō* to *phileō*.

When Peter expresses his hurt that his Lord has felt the need to repeat the question three times, Jesus ignores him. Instead of tending to Peter's ego, he solemnly warns him of what fate awaits the Rock: a cross to match the one upon which Jesus hung. This is the alternative criterion that the gospel presents in its final acceptance of Peter's leadership. It is not his holding of the office of apostle but his eventual (unwilling!) martyrdom. It is the laying down of his life for the sheep, a historical event by the time the gospel was written, that allows John to place Peter as the shepherd of the sheep. Only at this point in the narrative is Peter commanded to follow Jesus (21:19). Jesus had rejected Peter's offer to follow him to the cross on Good Friday, in favor of a later date (13:36). That date had come by mid-century. From the perspective of John's gospel, it is only when Peter received the "good news" of the way in which he would "glorify God" that his discipleship began in earnest.

It is precisely here that Peter "turns" and sees the Beloved Disciple, described in great detail in the context of the Last Supper and betrayal. Just as Jesus' "prediction" of Peter's martyrdom relied on historical tradition, so the question Peter asks Jesus about the Beloved Disciple relies on a similar tradition. In this case, it is that the Beloved Disciple lived to a ripe old age with the community. Peter's question is the voice of the apostolic churches—which enthusiastically embraced the "tactic" of martyrdom as a way of revealing one's discipleship to the world—asking about the authenticity of a gospel whose author was explicitly remembered as *not* having been martyred. Jesus' answer sharply commands Peter to mind his own business. In the end, God has different plans for different people. What is required by the gospel from church leaders is not *death* but *love*. The gospel's author is *defined* by this criterion. Leaders are to be given respect not because they hold offices, but because they generate love among the sheep and are willing to protect that love with their life.

Taken as a whole, then, we find that John 21 moves the church out into its mission with a sober recognition of how easily we can be led astray, either by the world's threats or our own egos. We are challenged with this reminder each Lent/Easter season, lest the intervening months weaken our resolve and muddle our clarity of faith. In the end we are all catechumens, ever preparing to make the commitment to discipleship.

—Preaching and Reflection Ideas—

Preaching Themes

1. Consider the temptation to lose one's first post-baptismal verve and to go back to one's old way of life. Share stories of "second" conversion, the moment "later" when faith pushed someone out beyond his or her comfort zone and into the world. Where might this community find the huge catch of fish waiting to be brought to the community?

2. Reflect on the dialogue between Jesus and Peter in terms of the difference between friendship and love. What challenge does this exchange put to those in positions of leadership in the church? Where might today's church leaders be called to go where they do not wish in order to show their true shepherd-love for the people?

3. Consider our modern ambivalence about evangelizing others into the Way of Jesus. Imagine how Peter, the peasant fisherman, might have felt about preaching the good news to those around him. Emphasize the gospel's form of true evangelization: the witness to the world of our willingness to lay down our life for our friends, not the mere speaking of words about Jesus.

Small Group Activities

1. Take some quiet time to consider the parts of ourselves that want to disappear back into acceptable ways of life. How might we be called to haul in a catch of fish from right where we are? Where might we be called to go that we don't really want to go? Invite those who wish to share some of their reflection. Close with a ritual that invites people to dip their hands into dark water (water in a dark bowl, or water with dark food coloring in it) while naming something they feel called to bring up from the dark into the light.

2. Discuss what it might have been like for the first community of Jesus' followers in the days and weeks following Easter.

Without any system of sacraments or established scriptures, how might they have carried on? What might their family, friends, and neighbors have thought about them? What choices would they have had to make in order to do what Jesus commanded of them? After some time sharing ideas about the time of Jesus, consider how we are called to carry on the story in our own time.

3. Consider the relationship between the Beloved Disciple and Peter at the end of the gospel. Invite discussion on how each person's understanding of John's story fits in with the bigger New Testament picture of discipleship. What might it be like if the church only had John's gospel to guide it?

Reflection Questions

1. *Personal:* How does my everyday life help protect me from having to witness to my faith? Where might I be called to go to show how my love of God is not just a private relationship but one actively involved in shining light into the dark world?

2. *Social and cultural:* How does our culture make it easy for Christians to blend in with the wider society without taking risks? Who are people in our world who have shown us an example of shepherd-love, whether in the church or in other parts of the culture? Where do they find the strength to take the risk of public love?

3. *Ecclesial:* How were we taught to conceive of the church's "missionary" activity? What feelings arise as we consider the prospect of "witnessing" to the world about the way of Jesus? Does our local church engage in this kind of activity? Why or why not?

Epilogue

Reading the Church
through Johannine Eyes

Nearly two millennia after John's gospel first circulated among Christian communities throughout the Mediterranean region, much has happened to give rise to the current shape(s) of the church. Many New Testament writings support a church order that resembles the Roman "household codes," which established a hierarchical structure within the extended family, the basic unit of Roman society (e.g., Eph 5:22–6:9; Col 3:18–4:1) The latest writings in the canon show a tendency toward the establishment of church offices (deacon, priest, and bishop, along with the now unused office of widow and possibly others; see, e.g., 1 Tm 3, 5) and hierarchical control of doctrine (e.g., Titus). Other writings seem to urge the establishment of a church that submits to secular authority (e.g., Rom 13: 1-7; 1 Pt 2:13-14).

Persecution of Christians by Rome in the second century hardened many of these attitudes. Church leaders preached a form of discipleship that both engaged in witness-unto-death before the empire and came down hard on those within the churches who preached "unorthodox" doctrine, such as the gnostics. If one was going to die as a Christian, the opponents ought to at least be clear as to what "Christian" meant! When Constantine's military victory-based conversion reversed Christianity's fortunes, the churches became shaped even more into institutions that fit well into the dominant Roman culture. Eventually, this process led to parallel and even overlapping European structures of crown and cross. The royal authority of the king was largely supported by the royal authority of the pope.

First with the Reformation and then with the Enlightenment, however, this hand-in-glove pattern began to unravel. Luther, Calvin, and Zwingli removed much of the glitter and pomp from their reformed church structures, greatly simplifying both liturgical practice and doctrinal teachings. Secular institutions grounded in the power of human reason gradually became divorced from church structures and authority. The monolithic, hierarchical structure of the one Roman Catholic Church gave way to a broad diversity of Christian communities and a wide range of secular structures that nodded in the direction of God and then proceeded about their business, independent of ecclesial control.

With the spread of powerful, modern empires such as the United States and the Soviet Union, which operated apart from churches, generations of Western people became socialized into world views that did not include the central authority of a hierarchical church. We see the results of this process in the United States today in the form of moves toward democratization of the church and the insistence on the full ministerial authority of women, married people, and gays and lesbians. It need hardly be pointed out that this has caused emotional clashes between defenders of the traditional forms of church structure and practice and those seeking to incarnate the church into local, more egalitarian cultural contexts.

What light might our examination of John's gospel shed on these struggles? How can we "read" the church today in light of our reading of John's story of Jesus and the Johannine community? Just as John's Jesus engages in both a critical and a constructive agenda in relation to the religious institutions of his own day, we can follow such a process in looking at the present and future of the church in our own day.

THE GENERAL STRUCTURE OF THE CHURCH

The fourth gospel provides no support for either a hierarchical or a democratic model of church. The metaphor of church as vine (Jesus) and branches (disciples) in John 15 is in pointed contrast to Paul's metaphor of a differentiated body (1 Cor 12:12-

31). In the Johannine model, *all* are branches, with the sole criterion of value being whether one "bears fruit." As we have seen, *apostle* is a verb, not a noun, in the fourth gospel. The authority of the Twelve is at most that of primacy of witness, not primacy of authority (6:67, 20:24). There is no hint or suggestion in the gospel of a call for members to submit to *any* human authority, whether in the church or in the world. All are "children of God," called to obedience solely to the Father of Jesus.

Furthermore, John's gospel provides no basis for a formal differentiation of function within the church. There is no mention of priest or teacher as official roles assigned to particular individuals or their successors. Eucharist and footwashing appear to be celebrations engaged in by the community as a whole, without a specific person as fixed leader. Munching Jesus' flesh and drinking his blood are signs of community solidarity, not occasions for ecclesial authority. In the same way, the intimacy that flows from washing feet is done by and for "one another." The gospel certainly looks toward baptism as the central ritual of initiation, but it says nothing about the who or how of the washing itself.

On the other hand, the gospel offers no solace to those seeking a democratic church, to the extent that this suggests modeling the Christian community on secular governmental institutions of voting, balance of powers, and so forth. Power, in the Johannine community, resides neither in the pope nor in the people, but rather, in the Paraclete. It is this Spirit who is both teacher and guide (14:26, 16:13). "Discernment of spirits," not power politics, is the Johannine means of shaping the life of the church (1 Jn 4:1-3).

John's gospel, then, presents a church that is radically egalitarian and pneumatic. The Spirit cannot be contained in ecclesial offices but blows where it wills (3:8). All members are equally capable of becoming vessels for the word the Paraclete speaks to the community. This is, of course, a wonderful model in theory and a very difficult one in practice: how does the community discern who the bearer of Spirit is at a given time? More than one discipleship community has come apart in dissension over where the truth resides.

Perhaps this is one factor in the fourth gospel's rapprochement with Peter, symbol of the apostolic model of church. For a given Christian community to survive the ups and downs of life *in* the world but not *of* it may well require a long-term connection with the apostolic tradition. But the emphasis in allowing for that connection is not official power but the authority that comes from faithful witness before the world's powers.

One implication of the radical egalitarianism of the fourth gospel is its rejection of distinctions based on gender, race, or class. If Peter is a "shepherd," the Samaritan woman and Mary Magdalene are both "apostles" (4:28-29, 39; 20:17-18). If the Twelve are noted as primary followers of Jesus, Martha is the one who speaks the titular "confession" of faith in Jesus (11:27). If Nicodemus and Joseph of Arimathea offer a form of honor to Jesus' dead body (19:38-42), it is Mary of Bethany who anoints his live body in anticipation of that burial (12:3). Whatever arguments are to be made in today's church for a distinction in roles based on gender can find no support in John's gospel.

The call to reject birth based on "the will of a man"—nationalism—also requires the rejection of racial and ethnic privileges of any kind. The inclusion of Samaritans and Greeks within the "elect" of God (4:3-42, 12:20-21, 15:16-19) breaks down any sense of priority grounded in the place of one's birth. In this way, the church is to be a model to the world of God's disdain for human-generated loyalties and identities that interfere with loyalty to God. This egalitarianism extends also to those otherwise rejected because of poverty, ill health, or other signs of marginalization. The fourth gospel's church is one where formerly blind beggars and others without official sanction can and must teach the privileged elite so as to save them from their own blindness (3:2-10, 9:34).

It has been said that Sunday morning is the time of greatest segregation in the United States. If we are to heed the word of the fourth gospel, we must face the challenge of constructing Christian communities in which multiculturalism is a fact of life, not a slogan of the "politically correct."

BREATHING IN:
THE INTERNAL LIFE OF THE CHURCH

While the structure of the Johannine model of church may be somewhat amorphous, its way of life is crystal clear. The three pillars of this life are baptism, eucharist, and footwashing. Through these acts of commitment and solidarity the gospel calls its members to a life of loving intimacy that provides the support and strength necessary to carry out its mission in a hostile world.

Baptism, in the Johannine perspective, signifies the commitment to a new birth, one wrought by God rather than by the world's powers. It announces the rejection of the "glory of humanity" in favor of the glory of God (5:44, 12:43). It marks the beginning of a new familial relationship through which one's fellow disciples become one's own flesh and blood.

In today's church the act of baptism sometimes is reduced to something akin to admission to a social club. While baptismal *theology* continues to proclaim the depth of commitment called for, the *practice* of initiation in a church surrounded by a dominant culture of materialism can seem like one more consumer choice. John's gospel underscores the radical break with the world that baptism is meant to signify. It calls the church to reject the shopping mall mentality that enables one to choose a church as one might choose a new pair of shoes.

The baptismal commitment, once made, is strengthened by the regular nourishment of eucharist, the "munching" of Jesus' flesh and drinking of his blood. It is an act suffused with neither magic nor mystification but with the joyous celebration of participation in the shared life of the Christian community. Baptism is the formal announcement of one's commitment to a new life; eucharist is the ongoing witness to this commitment.

John's gospel is the only New Testament document that speaks of eucharist in such graphic physical terms and contextualizes it narratively within a space of deep conflict and betrayal (6:51-71). In so doing, it presents eucharist not as a memorial to Jesus but as an act of public witness in opposition to the status quo. It memorializes the community's taking into its own body the broken and battered flesh of a Messiah mocked, scourged, and executed by empire. It calls the church to recognize its own vocation to become flesh for the life of the world.

This word was difficult to swallow when first announced (6:60) and remains difficult today. Eucharistic theology and practice often become caught up in ecclesial arguments about ministerial power (e.g., women priests or married priests), form and substance (e.g., the specifics of what constitutes "bread"), and ecumenism (e.g., who gets to participate). None of these issues would make sense to a church grounded solely in the fourth gospel.

The final pillar of the church's internal life, according to John's gospel, is footwashing. As we have seen, the common and facile interpretation of this ritual as a reminder of the Christian call to humble service does justice neither to the placement of the scene within the gospel narrative nor to the needs of the church, then and now. Perhaps the most difficult challenge of the gospel to the church is the invitation—indeed, the commandment—to develop bonds of intimacy among church members. Many U.S. churches consist of people who know only the backs of the heads of their fellow disciples, and perhaps the touch of a handshake. In a society marked by the freedom of many to choose and change at will the location of their home, employment, school, or church, the notion of developing long-lasting relationships of emotional depth and personal commitment may seem strange or even threatening. Of course, this perception is a relatively new one. It was not long ago that parish was coterminous with neighborhood and did indeed form a locus of relationships in which a church community worked out its collective call to discipleship. In our disintegrating social setting, however, footwashing offers an opportunity to restore the church's role of witness to the possibility of living in mutual love and support (13:34-35).

These three pillars of Johannine church life together constitute a "breathing in" that provides energy and life to the Christian community. Water, blood, and flesh—the primary constituents of human, physical life—are the vessels by which the church is born, nourished, and sustained. They fill the body of Christ with what it needs, not for its own sake, but to enable its mission to the world, the "breathing out" that completes the cycle of discipleship. It is to this final aspect of the church's existence that we now turn.

BREATHING OUT:
THE CHURCH'S MISSION TO THE WORLD

The church, at its best, has seen itself as living in service of God's *shalom*. The synoptic gospels characterize this mission in terms of the ministries (*diakonia*) of preaching, healing, and exorcism (e.g., Lk 9:1-2). John's gospel speaks of this mission in terms of the singular call to witness (*martyria*). Over three-quarters of the uses of the word *martyria* in the gospels are in the fourth gospel alone! It is the joyful act of public testimony, whether before the "court" of neighbor, bystander, family, or officials, that marks the Johannine discipleship mission to the world (9:8-34). The one who has been baptized is "sent forth" (*apostellō*) as a messenger of love and truth into a world filled with hostility, darkness, and violence.

Historically, of course, this act of witness was frequently twisted into acts of forced conversion and missionary imperialism. The ironic power of Christianity in the base communities of Latin America owes its origin to the slavery, plunder, and threats perpetrated on the indigenous peoples by European *conquistadores*. The gospel's challenge is the inverse of this practice; it calls disciples to accept suffering, if necessary, not to inflict it. It explicitly contrasts the violence that marks the world's form of conquest with Jesus' presence before the powers as a sheep led to slaughter (18:36–19:17). Fortunately, the church is discovering, albeit late in the day, that its encounter with the non-Christian "other" is to be engaged in with respect, love, and hope.

The act of public witness in the churches of our day has often been coopted by the image of door-to-door or street-corner evangelizing that marks the practice of some denominations. Alas, our embarrassment with this practice stems more from our absorption of the dominant culture's values of individualism, pluralism, and privacy than from an alternative vision of church mission. We do not wish to acknowledge—let alone imitate—the kind of public witness in which the Johannine Jesus is frequently engaged and to which he calls his followers. The story of his standing up in Jerusalem at the feast of Tabernacles to proclaim loudly his alternative understanding of the source of God's light and living water (7:37, 8:12) is rarely heard in today's liberal churches. It is not "polite," nor is it good "strategy." Yet it is crystal clear from our reading of the fourth gospel that Jesus not only practiced such an embarrassing form of public witness but commanded his disciples to follow in his footsteps (17:14-19, 20:21-22).

The basis of this witness, as always, is God's love for the world, as now manifested in the community of disciples (3:16, 17:20-21). Our liberal unwillingness to "impose" our values on others often masks a lack of true love for the world. This supposed respect for individual freedom mocks the interconnectedness of all life that is the nature of our createdness in God's image. Rejection of missionary violence does not imply a rejection of religious concern for the other. Rather, it calls for a steadfast, unwavering response to all who question our faith, as well as a bold proclamation of that faith in the public square.

Another aspect of the modern, liberal abhorrence of evangelizing witness is the fear of loss of social status that can accompany such acts. Not only does John's gospel express opposition to the desire to preserve one's social reputation (12:42-43), it goes on to claim that the nature of real love (*agapē*) involves a willingness to lay down one's life for one's friends, a laying down that occurs as the price of that love practiced publicly in the world (15:13-21).

Unfortunately, today's church has sometimes reduced this call to witnessing on behalf of a narrow range of social issues, largely involving sexuality. How different the church's life would be if its witness on behalf of the sacredness of life included a widespread testimony against the violence of war, racism, and economic inequality along with its witness against abortion and unhealthy sexuality! John's gospel offers little guidance in terms of the priority of particular social issues. Instead, it calls the church to witness to the presence in the world of the One who is life itself.

John's gospel is not the sum of the Christian tradition. Much of the church's structure and practice is grounded in other New Testament documents, as well as in the theological reflection of centuries of lived faith, hope, and love. Our reading of today's church in light of our reading of the fourth gospel is not intended to confine the church to the contours of the gospel but rather to enrich the life of the Christian community by listening to the voice of a particular gospel speaking to us today. In the end, the Beloved Disciple and Peter both have a role to play in guiding the church. The authority of both sources of wisdom, however, resides not in the power of apostleship-as-office but in the power of love-as-witness. As we continue our discipleship journey in a troubled and confused world, we can only hope that the Johannine memory of Jesus can persist in challenging the church to remember that *obedience* is rooted in *listening*, that prayerful openness to the Spirit who continues to blow, freely, wherever God wills.